BRADY'S
CIVIL WAR JOURNAL

Brady's Civil War Journal

Photographing the War 1861–65

THEODORE P. SAVAS

SKYHORSE PUBLISHING

Right: Sergeant Joseph Dore of the 7th New York State Militia leans on his Springfield Model 1861 rifle-musket.

www.skyhorsepublishing.com

10 9 8 7 6 5 4 3 2 1

Library of Congress Cataloging-in-Publication Data
Savas, Theodore P.
Brady's Civil War journal : photographing the war, 1861-1865 / Theodore P. Savas.
p. cm.
Includes index.
ISBN 978-1-60239-292-2 (alk. paper)
1. United States--History--Civil War, 1861-1865--Pictorial works. 2. United States--History--Civil War, 1861-1865--Photography. 3. United States--History--Civil War, 1861-1865--Environmental aspects--Pictorial works.
4. Landscape--United States--History--19th century--Pictorial works.
5. Soldiers--United States--History--19th century--Pictorial works. 6. Brady, Mathew B., 1823 (ca.)-1896. 7. Gardner, Alexander, 1821-1882.
8. O'Sullivan, Timothy H., 1840-1882. 9. War photographers--United States--Biography. I. Title.
E468.7.S285 2008
973.7--dc22

2008024983
Printed in China

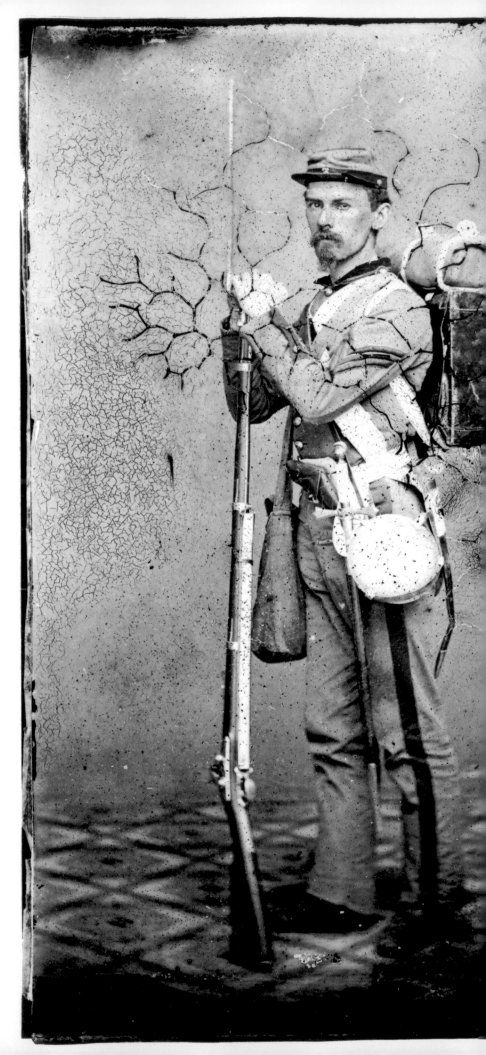

CONTENTS

FOREWORD

There are many reasons for studying the American Civil War, and people around the world have been discovering these reasons since the day the guns fell silent.

Some 600,000 Americans died during its four years of brutal, bloody combat—more than all of America's other wars combined. When the fighting ended, so did the tragedy of slavery in the United States. The war forged a still rather loose confederation of states into a united country with a strong national identity and a stronger central government; the conflict between States' Rights and secession was resolved at the point of the sword. The conflict was in many ways the first modern war. This is true not only because of advances in weapons' technology, railroads, or the telegraph, but because it played out in front of the unblinking eye of the camera. For the first time, the reality of the horrors of war was brought home through the new medium of photography, which captured the harvest of death in clear, unprecedented detail.

In 1861, photography was still a relatively new medium and nothing like the easy point and shoot method we use today. The first monochrome process of adhering permanently an image onto metal plates was only perfected in 1832. By 1850, the collodion process had become the primary means of preserving photographic images. Using chemicals to burn the black and white image onto a glass plate negative, the photographer could then transfer that image onto a cardboard card, called an albumen print. The process required the subject to sit still for several minutes while the image was saved onto the glass plate; even the slightest movement could blur the image and render it unusable. However, a properly preserved image had remarkable detail, sharpness, and clarity. The difficulty in obtaining a good clear image explains why capturing photographs of marching men or an actual battle remained beyond the technology of the day.

Photography quickly became more accessible to the public when cartes de visite were introduced to the American public in 1859. Developed and patented in Paris in the mid-1850s by a creative photographer named André Disdéri, the cartes de visite was a small photograph made from an albumen print, about 2 x 3½ inches, glued or otherwise mounted on a slightly larger card. The mass popularity in Europe of this style of photograph quickly made its way to the United States just a short time before the Civil War broke out in Charleston harbor in April 1861.

By 1861, most cities of any size had at least one photographic studio. The most famous of all belonged to Mathew Brady in Washington, D. C. Brady's early life is not well known. He was born in Warren County, New York, in 1822 to Irish immigrant parents, and moved to New York City

Opposite page: Union Soldiers huddled on the bank of Bull Run Creek, by a pontoon bridge, at Blackburn's Ford where the two Armies clashed at the first and second battles of Manassas.

about 1839 while still a teenager. Five years later he opened his first photographic studio in 1844. The art of photography was only in its infant stages during this time, but Brady managed to win many awards. Before long, he was renowned for his portraiture, both in the form of tin daguerreotypes or through albumen prints.

With the coming of war in 1861, Brady had a grand vision: he would bring the war to the American public through his photographic images. In order to assist him, he hired Alexander Gardner, Timothy O'Sullivan, and others to visit and photograph the battlefields. Each man was given a traveling wagon that doubled as a darkroom and sent out to capture the drama of the great national upheaval. The men returned home with stark images of death and destruction, some of which populate this volume. That they were able to do so with such remarkable clarity and ability still amazes to this day. Brady, whose eyesight began deteriorating in the 1850s, often remained at his headquarters in Washington, D.C., organizing the photographs and coordinating the efforts of his photographers in the field. This meant that he often received credit for taking photographs he in fact did not take, much to the detriment of the gifted men who actually labored in the field to capture those images.

In October 1862, Brady opened an exhibition of Gardner's photographs harvested from the battlefield at Antietam at Sharpsburg, Maryland. Taken shortly after the close of the battle, Gardner and his team captured for posterity a wide array of death and destruction. In order to save the loved ones back home as much angst as possible (and because most of the Union dead were already interred), he photographed only Confederate corpses in all forms of repose. The exhibit was entitled "The Dead at Antietam" and drew record crowds for days on end. For the first time in history, people on the home front were able to see with their own eyes what their sons, husbands, and fathers already knew: battlefields were terrible places, and nothing like heroic woodcuts and illustrations that routinely appeared in local newspapers.

Most of the photographs Brady processed and distributed, however, were not of the dead. Many depict the terrain where men of both sides fought and died, and showed the travails they overcame in the process. Their images captured nearly every aspect of the war, including railroads, bridges, ships, wagons, horses, buildings, and more. Common soldiers relaxing in camp or standing still on parade fields were favorites, as were images of the leaders of the Union armies.

For the public, however, the harvest of death images fired the imagination and remained seared in their memories forever. As he had at Antietam, Brady organized a post-battle photo shoot following Gettysburg, which once again revealed the terrible human toll that the conflict between North and South was claiming. This time, however, his cameras captured the dead from both armies—sometimes lying haphazardly on the field where they had fallen, sometimes in ragged lines where they had been gathered and only awaited the creation of a shallow burial trench. Perhaps the most famous image of all was the staged scene of a dead Confederate "sharpshooter" lying behind his stone breastwork on the southern portion of the field. The man was killed during the horrific fighting on July 2, 1863. Who he was remains a mystery that will likely never be solved, but the spot where his corpse was captured for posterity remains one of the most popular places to visit on the Gettysburg battlefield to this day.

Above: Mathew Brady leaning on a pair of horses that drew his photographic
wagon to the front lines of the various battlefields.

The images of Gardner, O'Sullivan, and their comrades offer us with many important lessons
about the American Civil War. Beside personalizing the men who fought that war, their
photographic images plainly show us the terrain features where they fought, and the effects of the
hard hand of war on the ground where the brave men of both sides march, bled, and died. The
careful study of these images teaches us what the historic appearance of the terrain looked like
during the time of the Civil War, and what we have lost in the name of development and progress.
They also help us better understand what Civil War soldiers experienced in a way that words
simply cannot convey. There are many lessons to be learned from these haunting images, once
again proving the truth of the statement that a picture is worth a thousand words.

The compilers of this book have done a fine job of choosing some of the most compelling and
illustrative images taken by the men who photographed the Civil War. You, the reader, can learn
many lessons from them, and I commend them to you.

Eric J. Wittenberg
Columbus, Ohio

Above: Mathew Brady as a young man during the time he had his photographic studio in New York's Broadway, which towered an impressive four stories high.

INTRODUCTION

Why Study the American Civil War? There is an overarching single reason why the American Civil War remains popular in books and movies, and why its battlefields are visited by the millions of tourists each year. Except for our long and bloody founding, the four years of strife represent the defining event in our nation's history. Whether everyone who reads its history and visits the hallowed fields fully realizes this in a conscious sense, they most certainly do in a deeper, perhaps intuitive understanding.

The force of arms was needed if large constitutional questions were to be resolved. The immediate question revolved around secession. Was it allowed under the U.S. Constitution, as many believed and openly advocated, or was the act of a state or group of states seeking to tear the union asunder unconstitutional? Our Revolution launched in 1775, argued many politicians and policymakers in the South, was not a revolution at all but the secession of part the home country from another segment. Contrary to popular belief, it was not the Southern states that first raised the specter of secession but New England! The states of the northeast threatened secession many times, beginning as early as 1803 when the Jefferson administration arranged the Louisiana Purchase, and again near the end of the War of 1812 (which essentially destroyed the Federalist Party). Three decades later New England rattled the secession sword again over the issue of Texas's annexation to the Union as a slave state.

Below the Mason-Dixon Line, South Carolina threatened to withdraw from the country over economic issues. Andrew Jackson responded with his own threat to invade the state with Federal troops, which triggered the resignation of a sitting vice president. South Carolina's threat was renewed twenty years later in 1850. The state finally made good on its warning when it withdrew from the Union in December of 1860, a breathtaking move that triggered a landslide of other states to follow in her wake–and the beginning of the Civil War. Only with the bayonet was the constitutional issue decided: The right of secession was not part of the original compact.

By why secede in the first place? The first eight decades of our existence firmly grounded original states–and those created during the intervening years–in two diametrically opposite philosophical camps: slave and free. Could a country erected on the brick and mortar of individual freedom and self determination continue with a large percentage of its population in chains? The war decided it could not.

A host of reasons were raised then and are still argued to this day in an effort to justify separation. The reasons span the gamut, from the nebulous "States' Rights" to tariff, economic, and social issues. But each of these was a lightning rod for war because each was tied to the institution of slavery. "[It] is fair to say that had there been no slavery there would have been no war," wrote a prominent Confederate general after the war. "Slavery was undoubtedly the immediate fomenting cause of the woeful American conflict." The country decided by force of arms that it would no longer tolerate slavery, and that decision was woven into our body politic by the 13th, 14th, and 15th amendments to the U.S. Constitution.

In addition to ending slavery and strangling the right of secession, the war profoundly changed America and its citizens. In the middle 1800s, most men spent their entire lives within a tight radius of their birthplace. But then war came, and young men from Iowa, Minnesota, and Massachusetts enlisted by the tens of thousands in a mad dash to avoid missing what most believed would be a short war. Boys from the rural Iowa prairie found themselves fighting in the swamps of Louisiana; others from big cities marched and died along the Mississippi River; merchants, doctors, clerks, and school teachers, North and South, were blockading Southern ports or manning the massive harbor forts, riding on the roofs of trains through a foreign landscape, or rotting inside prisoner of war camps. Many of those fortunate enough to survive returned home to begin their lives anew. Many others found they were unable to do so, and struck out West to tame new lands and uncover new adventures. All of them, whether they fought for the Union or the Confederacy, began their "second lives" with an entirely different understanding and appreciation for size and importance of their country, and their own small part in it.

The Civil War devastated much of the South, drained away untold millions for the engines of war, and left a bitterness that lingers to this day. More than 600,000 men died and hundreds of thousands more were injured in the effort to guarantee that the great American experiment would endure. What would the modern world look like if America had been cleaved in half by 1865?

And so I close as I began. There is a reason why the Civil War remains popular, why we visit its fields, why we struggle to preserve what is left, and why we teach it to our children. If we forget the defining event in our history that makes us what we are today, we will do so at the peril of our own existence.

PERSONALITIES

Like every major conflict throughout recorded history, the American Civil War tossed up a host of personalities who otherwise would have labored through life in relative obscurity. The bloody sectional strife brought every sort of character to the forefront of the public's consciousness, from capable generals to abject failures, to brave soldiers, pitiful cowards, and all manner of men in between.

The following pages display primarily a series of outstanding portraits of Confederate and Union officers. Most held the rank of general, although a few sported lesser rank. Even an admiral populates the gallery. Heroines for the ages, including the lovely spy Maria Isabella Boyd (better known as "Belle"), are also found here. Each had a part to play, for good or for ill, in the drama that unfolded day by day in nearly every American household for four long years.

Many of these personalities are well known to readers–among them Abraham Lincoln, George Armstrong Custer, and George Pickett. Others were dealt smaller hands to play, but play them they did with such dash and ardor that history still remembers their exploits. John S. Mosby, for example, carved out his immortal niche as a scout, partisan warrior, and dashing cavalryman operating with an élan that enthused Southern supporters as much as it enraged his opponents. Unwilling to surrender, Mosby simply rode home and practiced law. Decades later when he died in 1916, Americans were preparing anew for another war, this time in a distant land. While Mosby scouted Rose O'Neal Greenhow spied for the Southern cause. After enduring months in a Union prison for her activities, Greenhow traveled overseas, returning in the fall of 1864 on a blockade runner. Luck abandoned the lady spy off the mouth of the Cape Fear River when her small rowboat capsized. The $2,000 in gold she was carrying, money earned from royalties on her memoirs and intended for the nearly empty Confederate treasury, doomed her to the depths.

Right: President Abraham Lincoln (center) visits the Antietam battlefield on October 3, 1862, some two weeks after the guns fell silent. He urged his commanders to pursue the retreating enemy, to no avail. He is flanked by famed detective Allan Pinkerton (left) and Brigadier General John Alexander McClernand.

Above: Renowned Civil War photographer Mathew Brady (1823-1896) sits at far left among a group of fellow artists. After hostilities commenced in 1861, Brady determined to document the conflict in images. That July, he followed the armies to Bull Run, where he barely escaped death. Afterward, Brady mainly remained at his Washington, D.C. base, from which dispatched his numerous assistants–including Alexander Gardner and Timothy H. O'Sullivan–to travel the country and capture the scenes and personalities of the war.

Right: Brady poses for the camera. The New York native created over 10,000 images during the Civil War, at a cost exceeding $100,000. When the U.S. government refused to buy the plates, as Brady had expected, he was forced to sell his New York studio and declare bankruptcy. Though Congress purchased his photographic archive in 1875 for $25,000, the monies did nothing to allay Brady's financial troubles. He died, penniless, at the age of 73.

Below: Abraham Lincoln poses for the camera with his youngest son, Thomas, in 1864. Nicknamed "Tad," short for "Tadpole," Thomas was eight years old when the Civil War broke out. Though he had a lisp caused by a cleft palate, Tad was playful and outgoing, and helped infuse the wartime White House with life. He died in 1871 at the age of 18, after a brief illness.

Right: Abraham Lincoln's lanky, six feet, four inch frame is on full display in this photograph. Born on the Kentucky frontier, Lincoln became involved in politics at a young age, running for a spot in the Illinois General Assembly at 23. Despite many failures and setbacks, Lincoln persevered and built a name for himself in the newly formed Republican Party. At the time of his election as the sixteenth president of the United States, Lincoln was 51 years old.

Opposite page: Native Pennsylvanian Winfield Scott Hancock seemed destined for a military career. Named after War of 1812 hero Winfield Scott, Hancock graduated from West Point and fought in the Mexican-American War. During the Civil War, Hancock rose to the rank of major general and distinguished himself on many battlefields, including Gettysburg, where he earned the nickname "Hancock the Superb." After the war, he lost his bid for the presidency in 1880 on the Democratic ticket. He died in 1886.

Left: Famed Confederate cavalryman Wade Hampton was born in Charleston, South Carolina, in 1818 to one of the state's wealthiest families. He spent his early years on the family plantation, where he occupied his time hunting, riding, and receiving private instruction–generally learning the ways of the southern cavalier. He eventually ran plantations of his own, inheriting a vast fortune–and many slaves–upon his father's death in 1858.

Soon after South Carolina seceded from the Union in December 1860, Hampton raised the Hampton Legion, consisting of six infantry companies, four cavalry companies, and a battery of artillery. Hampton served as the unit's colonel, and in July 1861 led them into battle at Bull Run, where he was wounded slightly. Both Hampton, who rose to the rank of lieutenant general, and his Legion went on to distinguish themselves over the next several years. After the war, Hampton served as governor and U.S. senator from South Carolina. He died in 1902.

Right: Ohio native George Armstrong Custer may have graduated last in the West Point class of 1861, but he soon proved his worth on the battlefield. After stints as a second lieutenant in the 2nd and 5th U.S. Cavalry, Custer found his opportunity in late 1862 when he received a position on the staff of Major General Alfred Pleasonton. Soon awarded with promotion to brigadier general, the fearless and aggressive Custer developed into one of the Union's premier cavalry commanders, serving with distinction on numerous battlefields, including Gettysburg, Yellow Tavern, and Five Forks. At the time of his death at the 1876 Battle of Little Big Horn, in which he led the 7th U.S. Cavalry against a band of plains Indians, Custer was only 36 years old.

Left: John Singleton Mosby's youthful appearance belied his significant martial abilities. Born in Virginia in 1833, Mosby attended the University of Virginia, where he shot a fellow student during a fight, was convicted, and sentenced to a year in jail. Mosby took up the study of law during his incarceration; after his release in 1853, he was admitted to the bar.

When war broke out in 1861, Mosby enlisted as a private in the 1st Virginia Cavalry and fought at Bull Run. He thereafter scouted for Confederate cavalryman J.E.B. Stuart before securing authorization in 1863 to organize a band of partisan rangers to engage in guerilla warfare in northern Virginia. Mosby soon earned the nickname "Gray Ghost" for his ability to strike at the enemy quickly and elude capture. When Robert E. Lee surrendered his Army of Northern Virginia in 1865, Mosby, refusing himself to surrender, simply disbanded his rangers. He returned to the practice of law and died in 1916.

Right: As did many Civil War officers, George Edward Pickett began his military career as a cadet at West Point, where he, like George Custer, graduated last in his class. Also like Custer, Pickett soon however showed his worth on the battlefield, winning promotion for his bravery at the Battle of Chapultepec during the war with Mexico.

Pickett took great pride in his personal appearance–from his elaborate uniform to his perfectly coifed hair–and cut a dashing figure during his time as a Confederate officer. He led a brigade in 1862 during the Peninsula Campaign before receiving command of the division he would lead during the ill-fated "charge" on the third day of the Battle of Gettysburg that bears his name. The defeat at Gettysburg, where his men suffered appalling casualties, stayed with Pickett until his dying day. After the war, he entered the insurance business. He died in 1875 at age 50.

Left: Mathew Brady (seated left, in straw hat) poses with Major General Ambrose E. Burnside (reading newspaper) during a visit to Army of the Potomac headquarters. The West Point-educated Burnside, who entered the war as a colonel of a Rhode Island regiment, quickly rose through the ranks. After twice refusing the position, Burnside reluctantly accepted command of the Army of the Potomac in November 1862. He did not hold the post long; shortly after he led the army to disastrous defeat at Fredericksburg in December, President Lincoln removed him.

Right: Major General Joseph Hooker was Lincoln's choice to replace Burnside at the head of the Army of the Potomac. Born in Massachusetts in 1814, Hooker before the Civil War fought in Florida against the Seminole Indians and in Mexico, where he won laurels for his gallantry. During the Civil War, Hooker proved a controversial figure, not afraid to criticize his superiors-including Burnside, whom he called a "wretch" after the Fredericksburg debacle. Though an aggressive fighter and popular with the men, Hooker led the Army of the Potomac to yet another defeat, at Chancellorsville, in May 1863.

Left: Brigadier General Alfred Nattie Duffie was born in Paris, France, in 1835 and fought in the Crimea before coming to the United States in 1859, apparently hoping that his asthma might benefit from a change of climate. At the outbreak of the Civil War, he obtained a captain's commission in the 2nd New York Cavalry, then the colonelcy of the 1st Rhode Island Cavalry in 1862. Duffie eventually rose to the rank of brigadier general. Captured by Confederate partisans in October 1864, he was not exchanged until war's end. After the war, Duffie served as U.S. consul at Cadiz, Spain, a position he held until his death in 1880.

Above: Union cavalry commander Hugh Judson Kilpatrick poses for the camera in camp at Warrenton, Virginia, in September 1863. The New Jersey native graduated from West Point in 1861 and was wounded later that summer at the Battle of Big Bethel while leading a company of the 5th New York Infantry. After recuperating, he served as lieutenant colonel, then colonel, of the 2nd New York Cavalry. Before long, Kilpatrick earned the nickname "Kill-Cavalry" for his recklessness on the battlefield, his detractors charging that he regularly displayed a disregard for the lives of his men. Kilpatrick's performance during the Chancellorsville campaign earned him a brigadier general's star, and he commanded a division of cavalry at Gettysburg. Kilpatrick might be best known, however, for his part in an ill-fated 1864 raid on Richmond. After the war, Presidents Andrew Johnson and James Garfield both selected Kilpatrick as their minister to Chile. He died in that country in 1881 at age 45.

Above: When his native state seceded from the Union, Virginian Richard S. Ewell resigned from the U.S. Army to serve the Confederacy. He fought at Bull Run as a brigadier general and served under Thomas J. "Stonewall" Jackson's command in the Shenandoah Valley and on the Virginia Peninsula as a major general. After Jackson lost his life at Chancellorsville, Ewell, recently recovered from an amputated leg, was promoted to lieutenant general and put in command of the Army of Northern Virginia's Second Corps. At Gettysburg, his comrades accused him of delays that contributed to the Confederate defeat. Ewell survived the war and his bruised reputation, and settled into a farmer's life until his death in 1872.

Above: Congressman-turned-Confederate-general Richard Lee Turberville Beale served with distinction during the war, earning praise for his actions at Gettysburg and during the Overland Campaign of 1864. After the war, he returned to the U.S. Congress and the practice of law. He died in his native Virginia in 1893 at age 73.

Opposite right: Union general Louis D. Watkins and wife pose for Mathew Brady in his studio. During the Civil War, it was not uncommon for women to visit their army husbands at the front.

Above: Future First Lady Julia Grant, wife of Union general Ulysses S. Grant, and two of her four children pose for the camera. On the left is youngest son Jessie (1858-1934) and on the right is only daughter Ellen, known as "Nellie" (1855-1922).

Right: Arguably Ulysses Grant's most loyal and effective subordinate commander, William Tecumseh Sherman received great praise, and courted even greater controversy, during the Civil War. Despite a mixed performance as a brigade commander at Bull Run, Sherman received a promotion to brigadier general and a command in Kentucky. Feuds with the press and what some have called a nervous breakdown soon followed, as Sherman grew weary of the war. But after he received an appointment to Grant's command, Sherman compiled an impressive record of victories–capped by his famed "March to the Sea"–until war's end. Sherman served in the post-war army and died in 1891 at 71.

Above: William Mahone (1826-1895), a pre-war railroad superintendent, rose steadily through the Confederate ranks. Robert E. Lee appointed him major general for his conduct at the chaotic July 30, 1864, Battle of the Crater at Petersburg, where he rallied Confederate troops after Union miners tunneled under and used explosives to blow a massive hole in the rebel lines. Nicknamed "Little Billy" for his small stature, Mahone was with Lee at the surrender at Appomattox Court House in 1865.

Above: Mathew Brady took this photograph of Robert E. Lee shortly after he surrendered the Army of Northern Virginia to Grant. Lee was 58 at the time; he would die little more than five years later.

Opposite right: Georgia-born Joseph Wheeler's service as a Confederate cavalryman earned him the respect of Robert E. Lee and a promotion to major general. After the war, Wheeler volunteered to serve the U.S. during the Spanish-American War. As a sixty-one-year-old major general of volunteers, he commanded the cavalry division that included Theodore Roosevelt's Rough Riders.

Left: Brevet Brigadier General John E. Mulford (standing, in uniform) and his wife (in dark dress) pose on the porch of the Richmond home of the Allen family (at left) in April 1865. Mulford, who started the war as a captain in the 3rd New York Infantry, was at the time of the photo an assistant agent of prisoner exchange for the U.S. Army.

Above: Confederate spy Rose O'Neal Greenhow and her youngest daughter sit for the camera in 1862. At the time, Union officials were holding the widowed mother of four in Washington, D.C.'s Old Capitol Prison on the charges that she provided information, obtained from her connections in Washington, about the Union army to Confederate general P. G. T. Beauregard before the Battle of Bull Run. Greenhow was released after several months and sent to Richmond, where she quickly renewed her activities on behalf of the Confederacy. In September 1864, while returning from a mission to Europe, a Union gunboat approached the ship in which she was traveling off the North Carolina coast. Hoping to elude capture, Greenhow boarded a rowboat, which capsized; she drowned, taking the dispatches she carried with her.

Left: Like Rose Greenhow, Maria Isabella "Belle" Boyd used her considerable charms and guile to spy on behalf of the Confederacy. In 1861, at age 17, Belle shot and killed a drunken Union soldier who broke into the family home. Cleared of the charges, she began her life of espionage. In 1862, while Union officers gathered in a local hotel and discussed their coming movements, Belle hid upstairs and listened in through a hole in the floorboards. She personally passed the information she obtained to Stonewall Jackson at Front Royal, where, she told him, he faced a smaller force than he likely expected. Betrayed by one of her sources, she was imprisoned for a time. Belle survived the war and died in 1900 at 56.

Above: Rear Admiral John Adolph Dahlgren, commander of the South Atlantic Blockading Squadron, stands on board the USS Pawnee in this 1865 image. Beside Dahlgren is a 50-pounder Dahlgren Gun, a rifled cannon that he invented. This particular iron gun had a 5.1-inch bore and an overall length of 107 inches, and weighed approximately 3,500 pounds. Dahlgren's other invention, a boat howitzer that fired iron cartridges, found much less use during the war.

FIGHTING MEN

Tens of thousands of books and articles have been written on the American Civil War, but only a thin slice of those focus on all who made it possible: the men in the ranks. "Billy Yank" and "Johnny Reb," nicknames for the Federal and Confederate soldiers, enlisted with unbridled enthusiasm even as the smoke from the guns of Fort Sumter was still drifting above the troubled waters of Charleston harbor. Others were drafted in the first conscription in American history. By the time it was over, some 600,000 young men, North and South, were dead.

What prompted these men to leave their homes, their jobs, and their families to shoulder a musket and risk death, maiming, and disease in faraway places? Why men enlisted is still being debated, but martial enthusiasm, a call from one's state (or country), and a fear of being left behind as one's comrades left home to fight were strong motivations.

Despite the sickening horrors of war, nearly unbearable drudgery of camp life, and the filth and rampant disease that touched nearly everyone, most of the soldiers remained true to their oath, determined to see the war through to its conclusion. "I am sick of war," a Southern officer wrote his wife in 1863, "but were the contest again just commenced I would willingly undergo it again for the sake of . . . our country's independence and [our children's] liberty." A Federal officer felt the same, telling his wife he would not come home until the conflict was over. "[S]ick as I am of this war and bloodshed [and] as much as I want to be home with my dear wife and children . . . every day I have a more religious feeling, that this war is a crusade for the good of mankind. . . . I [cannot] bear to think of what my children would be if we were to permit this hell-begotten conspiracy to destroy this country."

These sentiments, echoed in thousands of letters home, help to explain why the bloody sectional strife lasted four very long years.

Right: Major General William H. French and staff gather in September 1863. A few months later, French would fall out of favor with his commanding officer, George Meade, who relieved him of field command.

Left: Two anonymous soldiers–of the roughly 2.75 million who fought for both sides–pose for the camera. The average Civil War soldier was white, born in the United States, single, and between the ages of 18 and 29. The majority of both Union and Confederate troops had been farmers before the war. By war's end, approximately 360,000 Union and 258,000 Confederate soldiers would be dead, victims of battle or disease.

Above right: A Federal cavalryman displays his weapons. Unlike their counterparts in the infantry, Civil War cavalrymen usually carried a combination of carbines (a short-barrel, single-shot, breech-loading weapon), pistols, and sabers. The mounted arm of both sides played an important role, from providing reconnaissance to harassing enemy forces.

Lower right: This wartime image of George W. Nailer, a non-commissioned officer in the 13th Pennsylvania Cavalry, found its way into a patriotic frame, emblazoned with the words "Constitution and Union." Like many soldiers on both sides, Nailer had his photo taken while away at war. Such images served as treasured keepsakes to loved ones back home.

Left: Not all Union soldiers wore blue. Here, a Federal infantryman dons a decidedly gray uniform. Various northern militia companies brought their own unique dress to the front, especially early in the war. At the Battle of Bull Run in July 1861, this diversity in uniforms led to great confusion between the two sides.

Right: Not all Confederate soldiers wore gray. Private Robert Patterson, Company D, 12th Tennessee (CSA) Infantry, strikes a confident pose in his dark blue-gray frock. He holds a single-shot pistol in his right hand; a bone-handled Bowie knife is tucked away in his belt. Patterson's regiment suffered heavy losses at the Battle of Stones River (December 31, 1862 to January 2, 1863), where Patterson was wounded. He lived a few days before dying in hospital.

Above: A stone mason before the war, Henry G. Hill enlisted in the 4th Michigan Infantry in June 1861. By 1864, when his term of service was up, he had reached the rank of second lieutenant.

Left: In the fall of 1861, twenty-nine-year-old William B. Hyde left his home in Albany to enlist in the 9th New York Cavalry. Soon commissioned the regiment's lieutenant colonel, Hyde resigned his position in June 1862 and joined the effort to recruit another cavalry unit in his home state.

Opposite page, left: A boyish Michigan infantryman strikes his best martial pose. Note the large Bowie knife and plaid shirt. In contrast to many spit-and-polish eastern Union regiments, those from western states often displayed a rougher appearance.

Previous page: A company of Union soldiers, bayonets fixed, pose in formation. Soldiers on both sides spent countless hours drilling—in squads, companies, regiments, and brigades—to learn the complex maneuvers required on the nineteenth-century battlefield. Note the drummer, who used his instrument to help keep the soldiers in step.

Left: Oscar Ryder served as a sergeant in New York City's famed 7th New York State Militia. At the outset of the conflict, the regiment, composed mainly of men from the city's leading families, mustered into federal service and shipped out for Virginia. After their three-month term expired, the 7th returned to New York, where it remained for most of the war's final years.

Right: Captain Charles Schwartz, a member of the 39th New York Infantry Regiment, aims his pistol at an imaginary foe. Formed in 1861, the 39th, known as the "Garibaldi Guard," drew its members largely from New York City's foreign-born population. It is estimated that one of every four Union soldiers was born outside the United States.

Left: During the Peninsula Campaign (March to July 1862), Major General George B. McClellan's advance against Richmond, the Army of the Potomac concentrated for a time at Cumberland Landing, Virginia, along the Pamunkey River, where Union forces consolidated and regrouped for the next phase of the push toward the Confederate capital. In this image of one of the many Union camps at Cumberland Landing, troops are seen formed in columns of companies for inspection. The tents in the background are thought to belong to the men of the 5th New York Infantry. In the foreground rests a mud-splattered forge cart.

Left: This photograph shows the men of the 44th Indiana Infantry's Company H. The 44th saw heavy combat during the war–including at Shiloh, Chickamauga, and Missionary Ridge–and suffered some 400 casualties due to combat and disease.

Above: Private Francis E. Brownell, 11th New York Infantry, killed the Virginia innkeeper who fatally shot his colonel, Elmer Ellsworth, after he entered the establishment to remove a Confederate flag flying above it. Brownell eventually received the Medal of Honor for his actions; the flag, stained with Ellsworth's blood, is at his feet.

Above: A Union infantry company on parade. As the war dragged on and casualties mounted most Civil War regiments found it difficult to replace the men they lost to battle, disease, capture, or desertion. Regimental strengths dwindled as a result.

Right: An unknown Union captain poses for the camera. Union officers had a much greater chance of surviving the war unscathed than did the men they commanded. Compared to their officers, enlisted men were killed or wounded in combat at a rate of approximately 16 to 1. They succumbed to disease at a rate of nearly 73 to 1.

Opposite page, right: These four Union Zouaves from Michigan pose with their 1842 model muskets. Many Union and some Confederate regiments outfitted their men in colorful Zouave attire, inspired by the famed French army units of the same name. Though the men pictured here do not don the baggy trousers typical of many Zouave uniforms, they do wear typically Zouave tasseled fezzes and white canvas leggings.

Left: Members of the color guard of the 7th Illinois Infantry gather around their national and state flags. Several of the men are holding Henry repeating rifles. Unlike the single-shot, muzzle-loading weapons carried by most Civil War soldiers that might be fired three times per minute, the lever-action, breech-loading Henry allowed its bearer to accurately fire its full load of 15 metallic cartridges in seconds. At the October 5, 1864, fight at Allatoona Pass, Georgia, the men of the 7th put their Henry rifles to good use, reportedly firing thousands of rounds in helping to thwart a Confederate attack. By war's end, the Henry had earned the respect of soldiers on both sides; one Confederate officer is reported to have said of the Henry, "It's a rifle that you could load on Sunday and shoot all week long."

Above: Five members of the famed Irish Brigade assemble for the camera in 1862. Among the group are two of the brigade's Catholic chaplains: Rev. James M. Dillon of the 63rd New York (seated center) and Rev. William Corby of the 88th New York (seated right).

Right: Unidentified Union Zouaves stand beside their weapons with varying degrees of enthusiasm. Not all who enlisted took to military life. By war's end, approximately 300,000 Union and Confederate troops had deserted.

ARTILLERY

The Civil War witnessed tremendous technological advancements. One of these was in the development, production, and use of the long-arm, or artillery. Although only a small percentage of men who fought in the Civil War served in the artillery, the long-arm of both sides was found on every main battlefield. Historians still debate the effectiveness of these guns. However, massed and well coordinated efforts, such as the Union batteries at Malvern Hill and Stones River, leave no doubt that, when properly employed, field artillery could turn the tide of battle.

A large mix of guns populated the armies and navies on both sides. In the field, mobile pieces ran the gamut from 6- and 12-pound iron and brass guns, to 3-inch Ordinance Rifles, 10-pound Parrott Rifles, and even the rare British-made breech-loading Whitworth Rifles–two of which were used by the Confederates during the fight at Gettysburg. Like shoulder-fired weapons, every field piece save one (the Whitworth) was loaded through the muzzle.

Smoothbore guns, especially the ubiquitous brass 12-pound Napoleon, continued to rule most of the battlefields. The Napoleon could hurl shells and solid shot nearly one mile. When under direct assault, these smoothbores were easily converted into giant shotguns by stuffing the barrel with a round of canister. This type of charge, a can of iron balls, blew apart attacking infantry. The advent of rifled artillery imparted a spin to the shell, which allowed gun crews to throw them farther and with greater accuracy.

New developments in casting massive artillery pieces allowed the production of seacoast and shipboard guns like the 100-pound Parrott, 11-inch Dahlgren, and 13-inch siege mortars. These "fixed" pieces were usually emplaced in fortifications or on board ships. Although many were mounted on swivels to cover a broad firing front, these big guns were not mobile like the smaller field pieces that moved with the armies.

Some of Mathew Brady's finest work included photographs of artillery, and many of the best of these are found on the pages that follow.

Right: A soldier from the 22nd New York State Militia stands with his weapon near Harpers Ferry, Virginia, in 1861. Two cannon sit in position behind him.

Left: Members of the garrison of Fort Woodbury in Arlington, Virginia, pose next to one of their big guns. The fort was one of a series that protected Washington, D.C., from possible Confederate attack. Collectively, this network of defenses was known as the "Arlington Line." Fort Woodbury, with its 275-yard-perimiter, had emplacements for 13 such guns.

Above: Another part of the U.S. capital's elaborate defenses was Battery Rodgers in Alexandria, Virginia, whose two guns—an 8-inch Parrott rifle (foreground) and 15-inch Rodman gun—overlooked a portion of the Potomac River.

Previous page: A close-up view of Battery Rodgers's Rodman gun, among the largest guns in the world at the time. A smoothbore that could fire both shot and shell, the nearly 50,000-pound Rodman required a dozen men to load and fire it.

Above left: A soldier poses for the camera in 1864 by fitting his entire body into Battery Rodgers's Rodman gun. The massive weapon fired 400-pound shot and 352-pound shell.

Left: The 1st Connecticut Artillery drills at Fort Richardson, Arlington, Virginia. Constructed during the fall of 1861 to buttress Washington's defenses, the fort, named after Brigadier General Israel B. Richardson, occupied the highest location about the capital. General Richardson would die the next year, mortally wounded at the Battle of Antietam. The 1st Connecticut would eventually leave Fort Richardson for the front; they saw heavy fighting during the siege of Petersburg in 1864.

Above: Union soldiers gather about the sally port at Fort Slemmer in Arlington Heights, Virginia. Typically, such structures were surrounded by some kind of abatis (usually felled trees) or a broad ditch or moat. A single, narrow entrance, sometimes equipped with drawbridge, also helped thwart potential attackers.

Right: Officers of the 3rd Massachusetts (Heavy) Artillery pose alongside one of the guns inside Fort Totten. Named after one the Union's most renowned military engineers, Brigadier General Joseph G. Totten, and located within a mile of President Lincoln's summer residence, the Soldiers' Home, the fort's 270-yard perimeter was protected by eight-foot-high earthen walls. During Confederate Jubal Early's 1864 advance against the capital, Fort Totten's 100-pounder Parrot rifle lent its support to the defense of nearby Fort Stevens.

Overleaf: This photograph shows a Confederate 12-pounder "Napoleon" cannon captured by Union soldiers from the 12th Maine and 17th New York Infantry regiments at the Battle of Hanover Court House on May 27, 1862. The reliable smoothbore cannon was one of the most popular and widely used during the war. Attached to the cannon is a two-wheeled carriage, called a limber, which carried an ammunition chest.

Left: This May 1862 photograph captures some of the vast quantity of artillery and ammunition available to General George B. McClellan's Army of the Potomac during the Peninsular Campaign. McClellan, whose massive force–over 120,000 men–had reached Yorktown the previous month, established this supply base on the Pamunkey River at White House Landing in May before resuming his cautious approach toward the Confederate capital. McClellan's campaign ended in failure two months later.

Above: Artillery pieces belonging to New York's "Excelsior Brigade" are lined up in storage at Washington Arsenal in the nation's capital. Ironically, the brigade's early commander, Daniel E. Sickles, was himself witness to the destructiveness of Civil War artillery: At Gettysburg, a Confederate cannon ball shattered his leg, requiring its amputation.

Left: These 13-inch seacoast mortars were some of the many big guns employed by General George McClellan during the siege of Yorktown, Virginia, at the outset of the Peninsular Campaign. Between April 5 and May 4, 1862, Union artillery lobbed thousands of pounds of ordnance a day against the Yorktown defenses. The mortars shown here could launch an approximately 200-pound explosive shell over two miles.

Above: This June 1862 images shows Captain John C. Tidball (second from left) of Battery A, 2nd U.S. Artillery, posing with members of his staff in the vicinity of Fair Oaks, Virginia. Later that month at Mechanicsville, Tidball and his artillerists, part of the Army of the Potomac's Horse Artillery Brigade, covered the Union withdrawal with their guns.

Above: Also taken at Fair Oaks in June 1862, this photograph captures the men, horses, and guns of Captain Horatio Gates Gibson's battery of the 3rd U.S. Artillery, also part of the Horse Artillery Brigade. Gibson and his mobile force were heavily engaged during the Peninsular Campaign; for his actions at Williamsburg the previous month, Gibson later received a brevet promotion.

Above: A collection of Army of the Potomac artillery officers–from the 1st, 2nd, and 4th U.S. Artillery–congregate around a gun at their headquarters in camp at Culpeper, Virginia, in September 1863. Roughly two months before, these men saw action at Gettysburg.

Right, above, and below: Union gunners demonstrate two of the many steps required to fire a cannon. Each member of the gun crew had a specific role. The gunner selected the range and type of ammunition, which others retrieved from the limber chest. Next, the ammunition was readied (fuses cut) and loaded, one man inserting it into the bore, another ramming it home. In the final steps, the gun was sighted and fired.

Above left: The gunners of Battery D, 2nd U. S. Artillery, work their weapons at Fredericksburg in 1863. A Union battery usually consisted of six guns, while a Confederate battery had four, though many exceptions existed on both sides.

Left: Union forces captured these cannon at Chattanooga, Tennessee. Confederate gunners under the command of Major General John Bell Hood operated them previously.

Overleaf: This photograph of a Union battery at drill demonstrates the number of men required to keep Civil War cannon firing. A captain commanded the battery (six cannon), while a lieutenant kept charge of each section (two cannon). Another officer was responsible for ordnance. Underneath them operated various gunners, drivers, and wagoneers. All told, each cannon might have 25 to 30 men and a dozen horses assigned to it.

Above: A Union soldier stands beside a modified 12-pounder Whitworth Rifle. This breech-loading gun, imported from England, was employed largely by the Confederacy, including at Gettysburg. Though an accurate weapon, the Whitworth's breech mechanism was problematic.

Left: For these captured Confederate siege guns, photographed in Richmond in April 1865, the war was over.

Right: This cannon formed part of a Confederate battery at Dutch Gap Canal, James River, Virginia. Photographed at war's end, it too would not again see action.

Below: This July 1864 image shows one of the rail-mounted mortars utilized by Union forces during the siege of Petersburg, Virginia. Rail cars could move these 17,000-pound weapons back and forth along the Union lines, depending on where they were needed most.

ARMY LIFE

Men in the army have always had reason to grumble, but for the average Civil War soldier, army life was boring in the best of times, and uncomfortable, filthy, and often deadly most of the time.

Developing massive armies to fight the war was something new for both North and South. Transporting the new recruits to large camps in order to turn them into soldiers was just the first of a host of logistical difficulties to be overcome. Clothing, feeding, arming, and housing the soldiers put a tremendous strain on the infra-structures of both sides.

With medical knowledge in its infancy during the middle 1800s, life in the army was often more dangerous than it was back home. As a result, the germ and not the bullet killed more men during the war. Jamming soldiers together in camps early in the conflict exposed them for the first time to a wide variety of diseases. Since most men did not have an effective immune system, the result was widespread illness and death.

The quality of food, which was often just this side of rancid, varied widely and was barely adequate to maintain health. Many men supplemented their meals by foraging for food and buying it from local sutlers. Religious health was seen by many as just as important as physical well-being. Camp revivals, church attendance, and regular worship routinely raised morale and kept men in the ranks.

Life in the army invariably included combat, and surviving a battle often depended upon the quality of the training. Were the officers experienced? Were they neighbors elected because of their popularity? Did they rigorously instill discipline, take care of the needs of their men, and require the best from everyone? Many soldiers griped in letters home about the strict discipline or endless drills, but the officers who required the most from their charges forged outstanding fighting outfits that knew how to perform difficult maneuvers under fire. As in all wars, good training saves lives.

Right: The men of the 2nd Maine Infantry mark Christmas Day, 1861, with a parade in their camp near Washington. Such events helped soldiers cope with separation from loved ones during the holidays.

Above left: Not all Civil War soldiers carried guns. Here, members of the 9th Veteran Reserve Corps's band pose with their instruments in Washington, D.C..

Left: This photograph shows the musicians of the 8th New York State Militia in June 1861. Many volunteer regiments recruited bands early in the war; by the end of 1861, more than 600 bands and 28,000 musicians accompanied Union regiments to the front.

Above: Three members of the 2nd Rhode Island Infantry pose with their drums. Drummers played an important role in Civil War regiments, their beats directing soldiers in a number of ways. "Reveille" woke soldiers in the morning, while "Taps" signaled lights out at night. In between, drummers beat calls for soldiers to eat, form for drill or parade, head to the hospital if sick, and to remain in quarters ("Tattoo").

Left: Members of the 93rd New York Infantry's drum corps stand with their instruments in camp. Note the young faces of several of those pictured. Regiments on both sides recruited boys to be drummers; thousands under the age of 15 served in the Union and Confederate armies. In battle, the drum corps bore the significant responsibility of communicating orders from officers and signaling various movements through their instruments, all while exposing themselves to danger alongside their comrades. Often when fighting broke out, the very young were sent to the rear to assist surgeons and to look after the wounded. Most drum corps also included a fifer (pictured at far right), who accompanied the drummers on his flute-like instrument.

Above: A soldier's life included plenty of downtime. Long stretches between battles—especially during the winter months—could lead to boredom, loneliness, and frustration. Here, four soldiers in full uniform bide their time outside their quarters.

Right: Soldiers on both sides spent their free hours in a variety of ways. These men of the 7th New York State Militia pose in front of their tent. Note the broom at right, used to tidy up, and the soldier (seated, far right) reading a newspaper. One appears to be writing a letter, while another smokes a cigar.

Below: Another group of Union soldiers–these of the 22nd New York Infantry–congregate in camp while off duty. Some are smoking pipes, while one appears to have put down a letter to pose for the camera. Standing at far left is a black boy, probably a contraband slave, who likely performed a variety of duties for the men of this tent, from cooking to washing clothing.

Previous page: A group of New York engineers display the tools of their trade and demonstrate some popular camp activities. On the left, one soldier holds a pickaxe, while another totes a shovel. A drummer rests at their feet. Next to them, two men sit at a small table, and another appears to be writing in a journal. Farther right, a man reads to two comrades from a book, while others stand ready by their rifles. At far left, a contraband servant holds a broom.

Right: Horse Artillery officers, and lady, pose in front of the headquarters building in their camp at Brandy Station, Virginia. When they had time, soldiers on both sides and of all ranks put great effort into constructing their camps. Especially in winter, when campaigning was limited by the elements, sturdy structures like these—made of heavy logs and equipped with stone chimneys— were not uncommon sights. Soldiers were known to lay out and name camp streets, as well as plant trees and other greenery to spruce up appearances—all in an effort to bring some of the elements of home to the front. Pet animals, like the dog by the officer seated at center, also found homes in many camps.

Above: Father Thomas F. Mooney celebrates Mass for an assembled group of Union soldiers in 1861. Mooney, the chaplain of the 69th New York State Militia, was one of the thousands of men of the cloth who accompanied the armies and saw to the spiritual needs of the soldiers on both sides.

Right: Brigadier General John A. Rawlins, army chief of staff, is photographed with his wife and child in the Army of the Potomac's camp at City Point, Virginia.

Below: Union officers–and contraband servant–pose outside their winter quarters. Though small, quarters like these brought some of the feeling and comfort of home to camp; note the glass window, shingled roof, and hinged door.

SUPPORT GROUPS

As the Civil War played itself out across much of the young country, a wide range of organizations supported the fighting men, the planning generals, the scheming politicians, and even the folks waiting at home.

Newspapers and mail played a key role during the war. While the papers offered local matters of import, many featured wide-ranging editorials about the course of the war—and soldiers devoured them whenever possible. Mail call was one of the most exciting times for soldiers, who were always anxious to hear from loved ones back home. Many newspapers also reproduced letters from soldiers at the front that today offer a goldmine of firsthand information many historians have long ignored.

Sutlers visited camps on both sides to sell soldiers everything from newspapers, food, clothing, and other items that otherwise were difficult to obtain. Their presence in camp helped boost morale and general health, as did photographers like Mathew Brady, whose tents for capturing images of the young American warriors were always popular attractions.

The telegraph was one of the technological developments that prompts many historians to describe the Civil War as the first modern war and the last of the old wars. This method of communication was an important means for transmitting not only personal news, but important military information. As the Union armies pushed South, teams of specially trained men strung telegraph poles and lines to enhance communications into the rear all the way to Washington, D.C. By the time the war ended, nearly 15,000 miles of telegraph wire crisscrossed the country—solely for official military business.

Legions of wheelwrights, blacksmiths, coopers, and mechanics traveled with the armies and labored largely in obscurity. One unique support arm that has received more popular attention involved the men who promoted and supported the use of hydrogen gas balloons—an early precursor of the modern air force. Although they were widely used, both sides relied upon military balloons to conduct reconnaissance. The most famous aeronaut was Thaddeus Lowe, whose Balloon Corps played an important role during the Peninsula Campaign of 1862.

Right: A vendor brings newspapers into a Union army camp in Virginia. Soldiers on both sides relied on newspapers for information about the progress of the war and goings-on back home.

Above: A U.S. military telegraph station at Wilcox's Landing, Virginia. From the time the first telegraph message was sent in 1844 to the outbreak of the Civil War in 1861, the number of telegraph lines grew steadily in the eastern U.S. The war brought an increased demand for the technology—both as a carrier of war news and a means of military communication. New lines sprouted up wherever the armies moved; by war's end, some 15,000 miles of telegraph line had been erected solely for military purposes.

Right, above, and lower: Two views of the portable hydrogen gas generators used to inflate Thaddeus S. C. Lowe's military balloons. At the outset of the war, Lowe, a prominent aeronaut and inventor, offered his services to the Union, which formed a Balloon Corps with Lowe as chief aeronaut. Lowe's balloons were utilized most notably during the Peninsular Campaign of 1862. The following year, a disgruntled Lowe returned to the private sector and the Balloon Corps fell out of use.

Overleaf: Workers pose in front of a government wheelwright shop in Washington, D.C. These men performed an unglamorous, yet vital, service for the army by repairing all variety of wheel-based military equipment, from artillery to wagons.

Right: This army mail wagon, and others like it, carried much-valued letters and packages to Civil War soldiers. During the war, hundreds of thousands of soldiers on both sides kept up a regular correspondence with friends and family. Army postmasters received and distributed incoming mail to the men and were entrusted with sending soldiers' letters home.

Below: Headquarters of the *New York Herald* in a Union army camp. Newspapers on both sides dispatched war correspondents to the front; their published reports kept readers informed of the latest military developments.

Above: Men of the U.S. Topographical Engineers pose outside their headquarters tent in Camp Winfield Scott during the Peninsular Campaign in May 1862. Both the Union and Confederacy employed engineers, whose duties included planning and constructing defenses, roads, and bridges, preparing accurate maps for military use, and scouting enemy positions. Civilian workers often aided the engineers in the construction of various projects; on the Confederate side, this non-military work force included slaves.

Right: Brigadier General Rufus Ingalls sits astride his horse in the Army of the Potomac's winter quarters at Brandy Station, Virginia, in 1864. The West Point-educated Ingalls, who began the war as an aide-de-camp to Major General George McClellan, became chief quartermaster of the Army of the Potomac in August 1862. He remained that army's chief procurer of supplies until war's end. During General Ulysses S. Grant's campaign against Petersburg in 1864 and 1865, Ingalls established and oversaw the massive military supply depot at City Point that provided Union soldiers with the guns and ammunition it used to defeat the Army of Northern Virginia.

Left: Members of Mathew Brady's photographic outfit pose for the camera near Petersburg, Virginia. These men would have followed the army on the march, safely transporting their equipment in the buggy and wagon pictured.

Right: Though the exact purpose of this "picture gallery" is unclear, it likely displayed photographs taken at the front. Civilians relied on the work of photographers to gain a sense of the nature of the war.

Below: These workers at a government saw mill in Lookout Mountain, Tennessee, provided the nearby Union army with the lumber it required.

Above: Military telegraph operators pose for the camera at City Point in August 1864. During the siege of Petersburg, these men ran lines throughout the Union lines, allowing the various parts of the army to keep in constant contact. Operators often came under hostile fire, especially when repairing line damaged or cut by the enemy.

Right: This photograph shows a U.S. telegraph battery wagon near Petersburg in the summer of 1864. Inside sits one of the wagon's two operators who were responsible for sending and receiving messages. Several orderlies also accompanied each wagon, which carried a portable battery that supplied the electric current on which the instrument functioned. These wagons accompanied the Union army during Grant's Overland Campaign, laying new telegraph lines wherever they went.

BATTLEFIELDS

The Civil War left behind hundreds of thousands of documents, but the greatest legacy we have today is the battlefields themselves.

Were it not for the meetings of armies large and small, once-sleepy towns like Sharpsburg and Gettysburg would not today be household names. Each offers a unique case study that educates us about the men who fought there and its impact on our history. Every fold of land, hill, ridge, valley, and tree lot played a silent, passive, and often deadly role in the evolution of a battle's tactics. Each leaves behind a distinctive legacy conjuring up images of duty, loyalty, honor, and courage.

The Civil War was the first conflict in history to be widely photographed. The war's most poignant images were those taken in the aftermath of a battle, once the armies had moved on. In their wake were the dead, strewn about the field in grotesque postures that both disgust and mesmerize. Who can ever forget the photographs Mathew Brady and others went to such great pains to capture for posterity, like the four partially buried Confederates who fell on July 2 at Gettysburg, or the crippled single tree at Sharpsburg with a silent grave at its foot? Both images, and many more like them, are found in the pages that follow.

The rolling pastures and timbered hillocks act like a siren song, calling to us from generations long gone. And we answer their call in massive numbers. Each year, some 2,000,000 people visit Gettysburg National Military Park. Many historians believe the Pennsylvania battle was a turning point in the war. The Union victory in early July 1863 ended General Robert E. Lee's raid above the Potomac River, often referred to as the "High Water Mark of the Confederacy." More than 50,000 Americans fell during those three days; many still remain on the field today in unmarked graves. Realizing the significance of the victory, President Abraham Lincoln selected Gettysburg to deliver his most famous address in November 1863.

Sadly, suburban sprawl and commercial development are rapidly consuming this precious and irreplaceable acreage.

Right: Taken from a mile away, this photograph shows Confederate soldiers in Fredericksburg, Virginia. As a defensive measure, the Confederates destroyed the railroad bridge in the foreground, which spanned the Rappahannock River, in April 1862.

Above: Alexander Gardner took this photo of the Lutheran Church on Main Street in Sharpsburg, Maryland, shortly after the battle of September 17, 1862. The church had been so damaged by artillery fire that it was torn down soon after.

Above right: Mathew Brady (left) poses outside Fort Beauregard at Manassas, Virginia. During the first battle at Bull Run in July 1861, Brady got so close to the action that he nearly was captured.

Lower right: Gardner shot this image, another of his series on post-battle Sharpsburg, looking northwest along Hall Street. The church visible in the distance is St. Paul's Episcopal. Like the Lutheran Church, it was heavily damaged during the battle. At the time Gardner took this photo, St. Paul's was being used as a hospital for soldiers wounded during the fighting. Note Gardner's photographic wagon in the foreground.

Right: Alexander Gardner did not only photograph damaged buildings during his visit to the Antietam battlefield. In this image, Gardner's camera captures a lone grave at the foot of a tree on the battlefield. Some 23,000 soldiers were killed, wounded, or captured during the day's fighting—the bloodiest of the war.

Left: This Gardner image shows the battlefield grave of 21-year-old Lieutenant John A. Clark of the 7th Michigan Infantry, who was killed during the Union advance into the West Woods. Nearby is the body of a Confederate soldier, whose body was left above ground.

Opposite page: Gardner's camera captures Confederate dead in the Sunken Road on the Antietam battlefield. The road, worn down by years of wagon traffic, afforded the Confederates stationed there a natural trench line, which they defended against repeated Union attacks, including from the famed Irish Brigade. Due to the level of carnage in this sector, the road soon came to be called the Bloody Lane.

Left: This photograph shows the Evergreen Cemetery gatehouse in Gettysburg, Pennsylvania. During the battle's second day, July 2, 1863, Confederates under Major General Jubal Early launched a night attack against this sector of the Union line, known as East Cemetery Hill. The Union defenses held.

Below: Timothy O'Sullivan, a member of Mathew Brady's photographic team, took this image of Union dead arranged for burial outside a Fredericksburg, Virginia, hospital in May 1864. These men likely were casualties of the fighting at nearby Spotsylvania Court House, where the armies of U. S. Grant and Robert E. Lee fought to a bloody stalemate.

Above: Mathew Brady traveled to Gettysburg shortly after the fighting ended to photograph the battlefield. He focused his camera on the various fields and hills over which the armies clashed, as well as on the battle's carnage–the still-unburied dead of both sides. In this photo, Brady strikes a contemplative pose for the camera as he looks toward McPherson's Woods, where Major General John F. Reynolds was shot in the neck and killed during the first day's fighting.

Right: Robert E. Lee used this stone house on the Chambersburg Pike as his headquarters during the Battle of Gettysburg. The building survives to this day, and is now home to a museum dedicated to the battle.

Left: These four soldiers lie where they were killed in the woods near Gettysburg's Little Round Top, high ground on the far left of the Union line, which was the scene of fierce fighting on July 2, 1863.

Opposite page: This Timothy O'Sullivan photograph shows an unfinished Confederate grave, possibly on the Rose farm, on the Gettysburg battlefield. When the responsibility of burying soldiers on the battlefield was left to the other side, the dead often found their way into hastily dug or mass graves that received little or no marking.

Left: Alexander Gardner took this photograph of dead Confederate soldiers on the rocky ground at the foot of Little Round Top known as the "Slaughter Pen." On the second day of the Battle of Gettysburg, Robert E. Lee directed part of his army against the left of the Union line, where it terminated at Little and Big Round Top. If the Confederates were able to occupy this vital high ground, the entire Union line might have become indefensible. Confusion on the Union side left Little Round Top unoccupied for a time that day, and Alabamians under the command of Colonel William C. Oates attempted to exploit the advantage. Union reinforcements reached the scene in the nick of time, however, and the bloody fight that ensued there—including the daring bayonet charge by Colonel Lawrence Chamberlain's 20th Maine Infantry—is believed by many to have saved the day, and the battle, for the Union.

Above: This wartime image shows the remains of men killed at the Battle of Gaines' Mill, Virginia, in 1862. The bodies of these and other soldiers– either overlooked or ignored–were not buried after the battle; they instead decayed where they fell.

Opposite page, above: A horse lies dead on the Gettysburg battlefield. Animals were not spared from the carnage of battle; at Gettysburg, an estimated 1,500 artillery horses lost their lives.

Opposite page, below: The bones and clothing of an unknown soldier are photographed after being unearthed from their shallow grave. During and after the war, the remains of countless hastily-buried Civil War soldiers were encountered on the old battlefields, often exposed after heavy rains.

Overleaf: This post-battle view of Missionary Ridge, Tennessee, shows the ground over which Union and Confederate forces clashed on November 25, 1863. Major General Ulysses Grant, who received command of the western U.S. armies the previous month, called for at advance against Missionary Ridge, high ground west of Chattanooga held by General Braxton Bragg's Army of Tennessee. After hours of combat along the line, Union soldiers from the command of Major General George H. Thomas braved Confederate fire and surged without orders up the center of the steep slope, dislodging all enemy fighters.

Above: A Confederate artillerist (foreground) lies dead in the trenches of Fort Mahone, Petersburg, Virginia, in 1865. Also pictured is a young black man killed during the fighting. Whether he was slave, servant, or civilian, we shall never know.

Right: This Confederate soldier, who met his end at the Battle of Spotsylvania Court House, Virginia, in May 1864, is thought to be from Lieutenant General Richard S. Ewell's Second Corps, who occupied the "Mule Shoe" sector of the Army of Northern Virginia's defenses. Over 30,000 men were killed, wounded, or captured during the course of the entire battle, which stretched on for days.

Right: A soldier is photographed while on picket duty along the Union lines at Petersburg, Virginia. Note the extensive trench lines; as the war dragged on, the armies on both sides built increasingly elaborate and extensive defensive works.

Left: A Confederate infantryman lies frozen in death on the Spotsylvania battlefield. Photographers were known to pose scenes of dead soldiers, repositioning weapons and accouterments–and even the bodies themselves–to make for more dramatic images.

Opposite page: The flooded Appomattox River, swelled by spring rains, as it appeared to U. S. Grant as he pursued Robert E. Lee's retreating army in 1865. The freshet delayed, but did not deter, Grant in his mission; he would accept the formal surrender of the Army of Northern Virginia within weeks.

PRISONERS

Prisoners have been a simple fact of life in every war. In the Civil War, neither side was remotely ready or able to deal with the number of captives that fell into their hands. During the war (and not including the final surrenders), more than 400,000 men were captured and spent at least some time as prisoners of war.

Initially, being captured usually meant nothing more than a delay in being able to return to one's unit. Following Western (European) historical tradition, Civil War soldiers did not, as a rule, kill, torture, or enslave their prisoners. Both sides paroled their captives with the agreement they would not rearm themselves until they had been formally exchanged. Since few believed the war would last long, prisoner accommodations were haphazard at best.

The strains and expense placed upon the exchange system only increased as the number of prisoners skyrocketed. Before the end of 1863, there were substantially more Confederates in Northern prisons than Federals in Southern prisons. When it was clear that the system of exchange provided a steady stream of reinforcements to the Rebel army, the policy of exchanging prisoners officially ended. Captured soldiers were sent to prison camps.

Some 150 different sites were used as prisons, North and South, during the war. Only a handful today are known by name to the public at large. The best known (and most infamous) was southwest Georgia's Andersonville. Officially called Camp Sumter, Andersonville was a stockade-style camp thrown together early in 1864. Although designed to hold about 10,000 POWs, by July 1864 more than 30,000 souls were crammed within its log walls. A stagnant creek that divided the camp provided the prisoners with drinking water while doubling as a giant open-air toilet. With virtually no shelter, starvation rations, and indifferent medical care, it is no surprise that nearly one in three men held there died. Andersonville's commandant, Captain Henry Wirz, was later hanged for war crimes, though much of the suffering there was a direct result of a failing Southern economy and grave logistical difficulties.

Right: This image shows the infamous Libby Prison in Richmond, Virginia, after U.S. forces took the city. A converted warehouse, the prison held Union officers and gained infamy for its unsanitary conditions and high death rate.

Above left: Old Capitol Prison in Washington, D.C. The building, constructed after the British burned the U.S. capitol during the War of 1812, served as the substitute seat of government until 1825. Afterward, it was used as a boarding house. At the outbreak of the war, the federal government took over the run-down building, turning it into a place to jail prisoners of war, spies, and deserters. Among the prison's more famous inmates were rebel spies Rose Greenhow and Belle Boyd, as well as Confederate partisan ranger John Mosby and jailer Henry Wirz.

Left: The brick building on the left, owned by the slave-trading Price, Birch, and Co., operated as a slave pen before the Civil War. During the war, occupying Union forces used the Alexandria, Virginia, building as a military prison.

Above: Interior view of the Richmond, Virginia, prison known as Castle Thunder. Consisting of three structures–converted tobacco factories and a warehouse–connected by fencing and brick walls, Castle Thunder primarily held civilians charged with political crimes, treason, and espionage. Also incarcerated were Confederate army deserters and captured Union soldiers. The prison, which held some 1,400 at full capacity, soon gained a reputation for its rough inmate population and brutal conditions. In 1863, the Confederate Congress launched an investigation of Castle Thunder's commandant, accused of unnecessary cruelty and inhumanity. He was cleared of all charges. When Union forces occupied Richmond at war's end, they used Castle Thunder to hold Confederates accused of war crimes.

Left: In this photograph, Union soldiers are shown guarding a long line of Confederates taken prisoner at the April 1865 Battle of Five Forks, Virginia, where Union forces under Major General Philip Sheridan overwhelmed Confederates from the command of Major General George Pickett, who was miles away at a fish bake when the attack commenced. The loss prompted Robert E. Lee to abandon his defenses at Petersburg; little more than a week later, he would surrender the Army of Northern Virginia at Appomattox Court House. This image of Pickett's captured troops shows them, minus weapons, as they would have appeared on the battlefield. Note how several curious Confederates turned their heads to sneak a peak at the nearby camera.

Left: The steamer *New York* awaits an exchange of prisoners at Aiken's Landing on the James River in Virginia during the winter of 1864-1865. Between July 1862 and May 1863, a system of prisoner exchange existed between the two sides, whereby soldiers were swapped according to rank (e.g., one colonel for 15 enlisted men). Though the system broke down, largely over how to handle captured black troops, the practice continued on occasion under special agreement.

Left: These Confederate soldiers, captured at the Battle of Spotsylvania on May 12, 1864, await transport at Belle Plain, Virginia. Prisoners remained in the camp at Belle Plain temporarily, until sent north to Union prisons at Johnson's Island, Camp Douglas, Elmira, and elsewhere. After the system of exchange failed, the burdens of imprisoning an increasing number of captives challenged both sides.

Above: Confederate soldiers captured at Gettysburg strike a dignified pose for the camera shortly after the battle. The chances that these men, and others like them, emerged from captivity alive and in good health were slim. Malnutrition, disease, and cruelty in prisons on both sides contributed to an estimated 56,000 deaths. Countless others who survived their time as prisoners of war would be plagued by a variety of ailments for the rest of their days.

HOSPITALS

One statistic that never fails to surprise people is that for every soldier who died in combat or as a result of a wound, two more perished from disease or some form of illness. This stunning mortality rate resulted from a host of reasons and, like so many things that transpired during the Civil War, neither side was prepared to handle the massive numbers of sick and injured.

Camp conditions killed untold thousands of men, many away from home for the first time in their young lives. Cramped camps, bad water, improper diet, and poor medical care weakened the body and spread disease among men who had not yet built up a proper immune system.

Medical knowledge in the 1860s was in a state of transition and only a handful of years away from significant advances that would have saved tens of thousands of men had the war been fought just two decades later. What seems elementary today, such as the need for doctors to wash their hands between patients, scrubbing tables, and changing bandages often to prevent infection, was not recognized in the middle 1800s. Doctors did not understand bacteria and the transmission of air- and fluid-borne diseases.

Battlefield injuries offer a prime example of the deficiencies of medical care. Amputations–often hastily performed by doctors unskilled in field surgery–were a routine method of dealing with badly injured limbs. Hospitals in the field consisted of anything able to hold a wounded man, including filthy barns, tents, and houses. More often than not, men spent days in the open in all kinds of weather before and after surgery. As a result, if a wound did not directly kill the soldier, the infection (or medical treatment) that routinely followed often did.

The means of transportation was also hard on the unfortunate wounded, who were usually carried to a medical facility inside a jolting, bumpy wagon or via stretcher. The journey was always painful and dangerous, and sometimes hastened death by tearing open or aggravating wounds. Given the hazards encountered during the war, simply making it out alive was an achievement too few recognize today.

Right: This undated image shows the hospital of the U.S. Quartermaster Department located in Washington, D. C. Note the ambulance wagon parked outside the gate.

Above: This Alexandria, Virginia, facility was one of many maintained by the U.S. Sanitary Commission (USSC) during the Civil War. Founded in 1861, the USSC enlisted an army of civilian volunteers who dedicated themselves to improving the condition of soldiers by promoting good health and hygiene in camps and hospitals. USCC members raised funds to provide soldiers with food and supplies, staffed hospitals for ailing troops, and assisted veterans in their quest for back pay and pensions. Women played a key role in the organization, which disbanded after the war in 1866.

Right: In June 1862, the medical staff of Brigadier General Joseph Hooker's division used this house, located on the battlefield at Fair Oaks, Virginia, as a hospital to treat soldiers wounded during the fighting. Both sides regularly commandeered nearby buildings–including churches–for use as temporary hospitals during and after battles. Soldiers who survived their wounds were eventually shipped to larger medical facilities.

Overleaf: This 1862 photograph shows members of the newly formed U.S. Ambulance Corps demonstrating how sick or wounded soldiers were removed from the field. Here, orderlies in Zouave dress use stretchers to carry men to a horse-drawn ambulance wagon. A medical officer (with sword) stands to the left of the activity. On the ambulance, canvas curtains (rolled up in this photograph) could be lowered for protection from the elements or privacy. Seats up front permitted hospital stewards to ride along with their patients. Though not seen here, many wagons carried water kegs underneath the carriage.

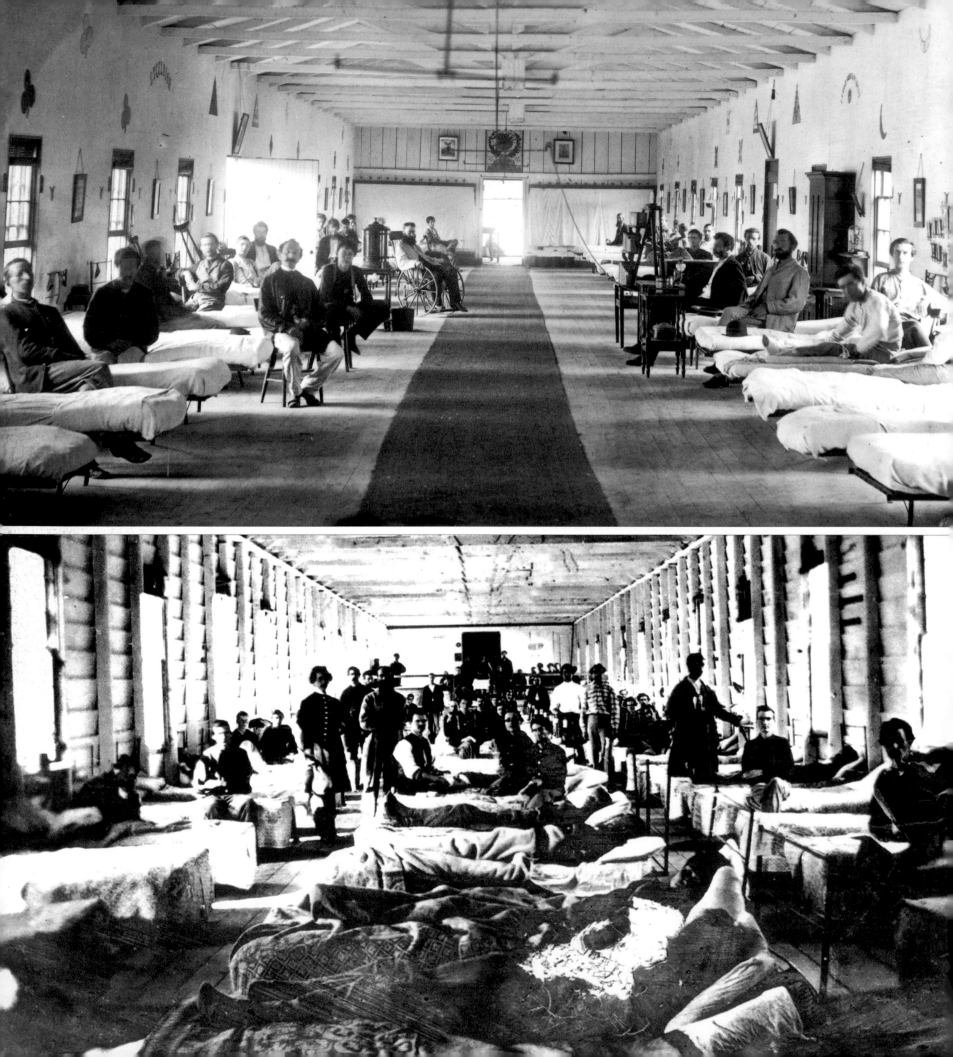

Above left: This image shows patients in Armory Square Hospital's Ward K in 1865. Constructed in 1862 on the National Mall in Washington, D.C., the hospital boasted 1,000 beds as well as several overflow tents with which to house additional patients. Also included in the complex were a chapel and officers' quarters.

Left: Sick and wounded Union soldiers crowd this hospital ward in a convalescent camp at Alexandria, Virginia. Such structures often were converted regimental barracks, vacated when an army pulled up stakes for the front. Those patients well enough might be put to work in camp. All fought boredom in addition to their ailments.

Above: These convalescing Union soldiers look to the camera from their beds at Harewood General Hospital in Washington, D.C. Note how each bed has its own mosquito-netting that could be drawn to cover the patient. These nets were likely put in place to keep away pesky insects, not to protect from sickness, as people of the time did not fully understand the nature of insect-borne disease, which wreaked havoc on the armies. Some two-thirds of the over 350,000 Union soldiers who died during the war succumbed to disease, not enemy fire.

Above: A woman's nursing corps was formed to distribute comfort to the wounded. Famous nurse Clara Barton who traveled with the Union army ambulances tending the sick for over three years, went on to found the American Red Cross in 1881.

Right: Convalescing Union soldiers pose for the camera in a "rest house" maintained by the U.S. Sanitary Commission in Washington, D.C. The USSC opened many such facilities, which offered Union soldiers in need a temporary bed and good meal as they made their way homeward.

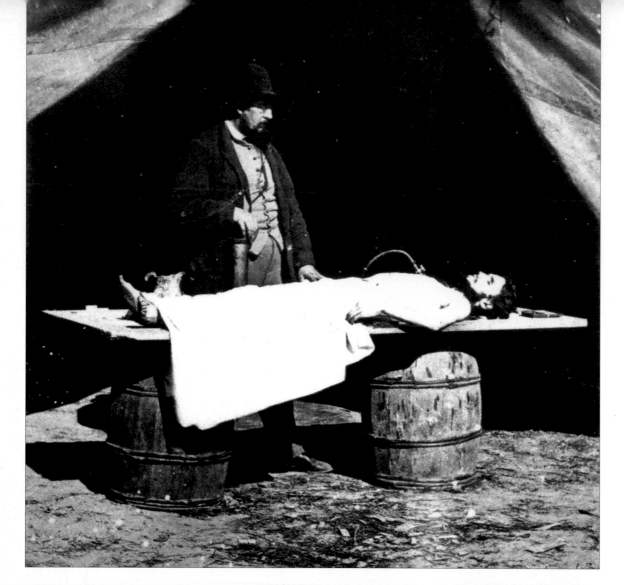

Left: Dr. Richard Burr, an embalming surgeon, works on an unknown soldier's body. Embalming was a popular procedure during the war, as countless families wished the remains of their loved ones preserved for services and burial at home. Burr and other embalmers practiced arterial embalming, whereby they filled deceased soldiers' veins with a chemical preservative.

Right: Union soldiers wounded during the fighting at Spotsylvania Court House, Virginia, in May 1864, rest on the ground outside a field hospital.

Below: Faced with a lack of space, authorities at Douglas Hospital in Washington, D.C. set up rows of tents on hospital grounds to house an overflow of convalescents.

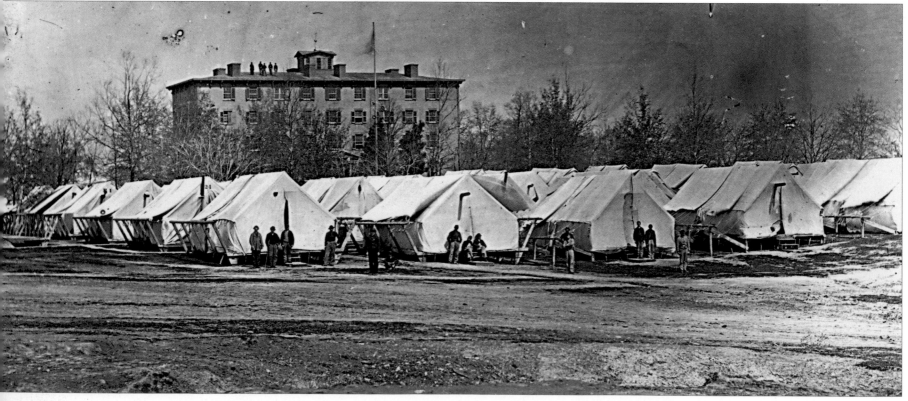

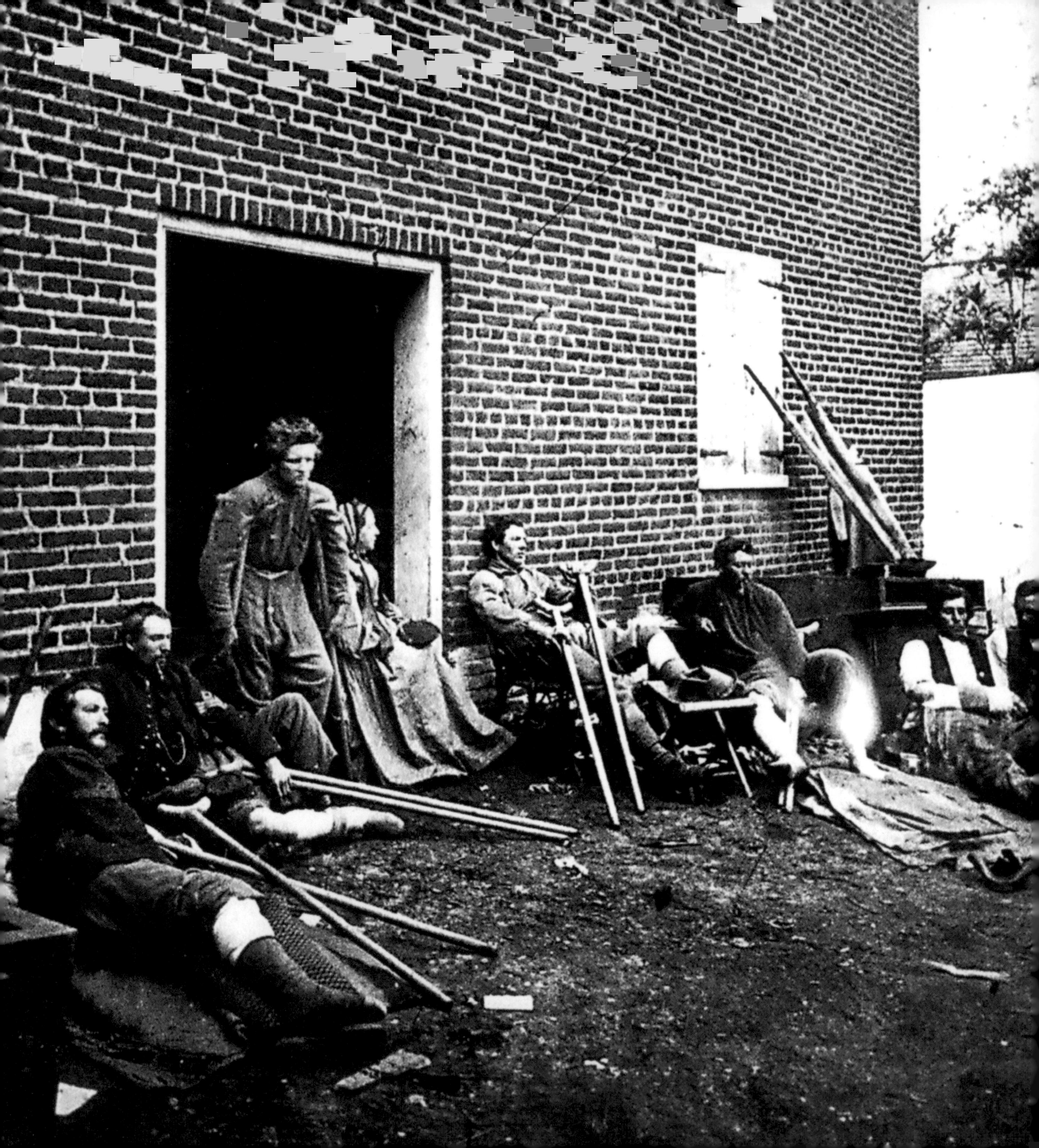

Left: A Sanitary Commission nurse checks on soldiers recuperating at a Fredericksburg, Virginia, field hospital. These men were among the thousands of Union troops wounded during U.S. Grant's Overland Campaign in 1864.

Above: Civil War surgeons occasionally found themselves exposed to enemy fire. At Petersburg in April 1865, Dr. William R. D. Blackwood (seated center) dashed between the lines to retrieve comrades wounded during heavy fighting. Though Confederate artillery shells landed all around him, the doctor returned to Union lines unscathed. Blackwood was later awarded the Medal of Honor for gallantry.

Left: Wounded Union soldiers recuperate at a field hospital on Marye's Heights, Fredericksburg, after fighting in May 1864. Left of the tree rest two Indians, likely members of Company K, 1st Michigan Sharpshooters. Over 20,000 Native Americans fought on both sides during the war.

Above: An assemblage of hospital stewards from the Second Division, Ninth Corps, Army of the Potomac pose for the camera in October 1864. Stewards fulfilled a variety of roles. They assisted surgeons at the front, dispensing medicines and dressing minor wounds. Stewards also oversaw the administration of field hospitals and kept track of medical supplies. In addition, they were charged with the duty of extracting soldiers' aching teeth.

FORTIFICATIONS

Fortifications have played a role in nearly every war throughout recorded history. One of the most famous early examples took place in 52 B.C. in Gaul, where Caesar erected a massive line of double-faced works around Alesia, pinning Vercingetorix and his Gallic warriors inside. In our own Civil War, the initial outbreak of fighting swirled around a masonry fort in the center of Charleston harbor. In Virginia, the Civil War drew to close at Appomattox Courthouse on April 9, 1865, just a little more than one week after what was left of Robert E. Lee's Army of Northern Virginia was driven out of what historian Ear1 J. Hess described as the "most sophisticated system of field fortifications yet seen in the history of the world." Caesar would not have felt terribly out of place walking Lee's final lines around Petersburg.

During the war's early years, most soldiers and their generals looked with disdain upon the idea that men should dig in to protect themselves on the battlefield. Some believed that digging in was cowardly—a demonstrated unwillingness to come to grips with the enemy. Others believed that fighting behind entrenchments dulled the offensive spirit that was so imperative to winning the war. As the war dragged on, soldiers realized the benefits of a wall of earth, and used everything from shovels and tin cups to bayonets and bare hands to make themselves safer from enemy lead and iron.

Fortifications came in all shapes and sizes, from massive masonry bastions like Forts Sumter and Monroe, to sprawling coastal defensives, entrenchments protecting railroads and bridges, formal siege works (such as described above at Petersburg), and open field fortifications of the kind thrown up by the opposing armies in Virginia during the Overland Campaign of 1864.

Only now is the design, implementation, and impact of fortifications on specific battles and campaigns being seriously studied. Thankfully, some of the finest photographs to come out of the Civil War—including images of magnificent trench systems—are found in the pages that follow.

Right: The Confederate fortifications pictured here defended the city of Atlanta from Major General William T. Sherman's advancing Union forces in 1864. A cavalryman belonging to Sherman's victorious army stands near the captured rebel guns.

Above: This photograph shows the main entrance to Fort Monroe, located at Old Point Comfort on the tip of the Virginia Peninsula. Completed in 1834, the hexagon-shaped fort was completely surrounded by a moat and accommodated hundreds of cannon. Between 1865 and 1867, former Confederate president Jefferson Davis was imprisoned here.

Right: Union soldiers mill about this abandoned Confederate fortification at Yorktown, Virginia. As Major General George McClellan's army advanced up the Virginia Peninsula in 1862, Confederate commander John Magruder's outmanned and outgunned force utilized an impressive system of fortifications to slow the Union advance. Note the destroyed rebel cannon.

Below: Fort Moultrie, located on Sullivan's Island, South Carolina, was one of four forts that protected Charleston Harbor from enemy incursion. In this interior shot of Moultrie, neatly stacked piles of cannon balls rest near the fort's shot-heating furnace. Artillerists heated the iron shot for use against wooden targets (ships or fortifications) in hopes of starting fires.

Left: This interior shot of the Union's Fort Sedgwick highlights a section of its formidable gabion entrenchments and (outside the walls, in background) abatis. During the Petersburg Campaign, the Confederates stationed across the lines dubbed Sedgwick "Fort Hell" for the incessant and deadly artillery fire that emanated from its walls.

Above: A soldier sits atop a pile of fascines, or bundles of sticks, of the type used to construct the gabion behind him. Stood on end, filled with earth, and topped by sandbags (as shown here), gabions were used by both sides at Petersburg to create extremely strong defenses.

Left: These Union soldiers pose for the camera outside the entrance to the powder magazine at Fort Brady. U.S. forces built this structure in the fall of 1864 as part of their attempt to neutralize the Confederate defenses on the James River at Drewry's Bluff. Note the use of gabions and heavy logs to strengthen this vital—and combustible—spot in the fort.

Above: Soldiers from Major General Benjamin Butler's Army of the James place 10-inch mortars into position along their lines at Dutch Gap, Virginia, in 1864. Note the lookout tower in the background. Soldiers used such structures to observe enemy positions and to communicate, via signal flags, along their own lines.

Previous page: A group of Union soldiers take a break from the hard work of digging breastworks outside Petersburg, Virginia. The opposing armies at Petersburg constructed mile after mile of defensive works like these, foreshadowing the trench warfare that would characterize the First World War.

Above: This heavily reinforced structure, known as a "bomb-proof,"
served as officers' quarters in the Union's Fort Sedgwick at
Petersburg. A series of gabions and sandbags, buttressed by many feet
of packed earth, protected its inhabitants from incoming enemy shells.

Left: Union soldiers pose outside the entrance to bombproof quarters in Fort Burnham. In September 1864, U.S. forces captured the fortification, formerly known as Fort Harrison, from the Confederates.

Below: These abandoned trenches formed part of Robert E. Lee's defensive network that circled the embattled city of Petersburg, Virginia, in 1864 and 1865. After ten months of bloody clashes with U.S. Grant's larger force, the stalemate ended when Grant broke through Lee's line in early April 1865, beginning a retreat that would end at Appomattox on April 9. An estimated 70,000 Union and Confederate soldiers were killed, wounded, or captured during the campaign.

FIGHTING SHIPS

Naval aspects of the Civil War played an integral role in shaping the strategy that preserved the Union. Yet, the war that played out along thousands of miles of Southern coastline and upon every major river system is routinely ignored or glossed over in most books.

Neither side was ready to fight a major war on the water. Shortly after the firing on Fort Sumter, President Lincoln declared a blockade of Confederate ports on April 19, 1861. His directive called for monitoring more than 3,000 miles of coastline and the closure of a dozen major ports. Lincoln's prime objective was to strangle the South by limiting its imports and the export of cotton. The Federal navy, however, had fewer than 50 ships ready for service when war broke out. Hundreds more, requiring many thousands of sailors, were commissioned for the grand undertaking. In an effort to combat this cordon, the Confederacy commissioned large numbers of private "blockade runners" to slip through the Union blockade with cotton and return with arms, ammunitions, and goods desperately needed by the Confederacy. Hundreds of these private ships were lost and the South's export of cotton dropped dramatically as the war progressed, crippling the Southern economy.

With only a handful of ships in 1861 and few resources, Confederate Secretary of the Navy Stephen Mallory relied upon technological innovations that included ironclads, fast torpedo "David" boats, mines, and even submarines. A remarkable achievement was the design, construction, and operation of the *CSS Hunley*, an iron submersible that sank the *USS Housatonic* off Charleston in the spring of 1864. The South launched dozens of ironclads, many on inland rivers to help block access into the heartland of the Confederacy. The most famous of these iron monsters was the *CSS Virginia* (popularly known as *Merrimack*). Its duel with the Union ironclad *Monitor* in Hampton Roads in March 1862 revolutionized naval warfare forever.

Whether steam- or wind-driven, fighting on the high seas, along the coast, or on a narrow muddy inland river, the naval war shaped the course and scope of the Civil War in ways few people today fully understand.

Right: At this wharf, coal-burning ships of the Union navy docked to restock their fuel supplies. Note the piles of coal positioned at various points.

Above left: Union naval personnel pose for the camera on the deck of the Confederate ram *Atlanta*, which fell to U.S. forces in June 1863. Originally a merchant steamship named *Fingal*, in early 1862 the Confederates began converting her into an ironclad; among her new armaments were iron plating and a heavy ram. In early 1864, the Union navy commissioned the captured *Atlanta* for its own use.

Lower left: Union soldiers observe vessels crowded along the Pamunkey River in Virginia. A tributary of the York River, the Pamunkey was the site of much activity during the Civil War. During the Peninsular Campaign, George McClellan used White House Landing on the river as a major supply base.

Above: Two Union sailors pose on the deck of a gunboat. By war's end, the size of the Union navy grew to include over 50,000 sailors, up from the approximately 7,000 who manned the U.S. fleet in 1861.

Overleaf: These three army tugs—numbered 3, 4, and 5—are shown at work on the James River in 1864. The U.S. monitor *Onondaga* is visible at rest in the background. The James bustled with activity during the siege of Petersburg, when U. S. Grant established his headquarters at the port town called City Point.

Left: U.S. naval officer W. N. Jeffers strikes a contemplative pose on the deck of the *USS Monitor*. Jeffers replaced John Worden in command of the famed ironclad after the latter was wounded during the ship's fight with the *CSS Virginia* in March 1862.

Right: Crewmen from the *HMS Nile* pose in Mathew Brady's studio. The *Nile* was flagship of the Royal Navy's North American Squadron; if England had entered the war, *Nile* likely would have seen action in it.

Below: Officers from the *USS Monitor* pose on the ship's deck. This vessel, the first in the U.S. fleet of monitor-class warships, saw less than a year's service before sinking off the North Carolina coast in December 1862.

Left: Union sailors crowd the deck of a federal gunboat. Compared to their brethren in the Union army, who enlisted from across the country and were primarily farmers before the war, sailors came overwhelmingly from urban areas along the east coast. An estimated 45 percent of Union sailors were born outside the U.S., whereas only 25 percent of Union soldiers were immigrants. Note the presence of boys and black men in this image. During the war blacks—both freemen and former slaves—served in growing numbers aboard Union ships, and boys occupied a number of roles, from servants and apprentices to powder monkeys—a job that entailed fetching powder from the ship's magazine and running it to the guns during battle.

Above: Famous photographer Mathew Brady (at left, in white coat) poses for the camera with a Union vessel behind him.

Right: Signalmen from Rear Admiral John A. Dahlgren's flagship display the tools of their trade. A ship's signal crew was responsible for sending and receiving communications via signal flags. With use of a telescopic lens (shown here on a tripod), ships could communicate at extended distances, even with allied forces on land.

Overleaf: Union sailors man a Dahlgren smoothbore cannon on board a Union gunship. Each man had a specific role to play in loading and firing the weapon. At right are the tools needed to cool and clean the barrel as well as ram home charges. With the aid of the ropes and pulleys shown, the men were able to position the gun before and after firing.

Above: This rear view of a ship's gun shows the carriage on which it was mounted. Note the carriage wheels, which permitted the gun to be replaced into firing position after recoiling during firing. Gunners used the screw at the back to alter their weapon's elevation.

Right: The USS *Galena*, one of the three kinds of ironclad ship commissioned by the U.S. government in 1861. Launched in February 1862, the 210-foot vessel carried six guns and was covered in three-inch iron plating on the sides. These armaments proved insufficient, however. After the *Galena* took heavy damage in battle, she was converted back into a wooden gunboat.

Below: The *USS St. Louis*, commissioned in January 1862, was an ironclad river gunboat that saw action that February during the fights for Forts Henry and Donelson, where she received heavy damage. Later that year, the *St. Louis* participated in actions against Confederate fortifications on the Mississippi River. Renamed *Baron de Kalb* in September, she sank after hitting a Confederate mine in July 1863.

Right: Broadway Landing, a key Union supply depot on the Appomattox River, bustles with activity in this wartime photograph. In 1864, Union forces under Major General Benjamin Butler constructed a lengthy pontoon bridge at Broadway, enabling them to cross the river on their advance toward the city of Petersburg. In this image, a number of supply ships are seen docked at Broadway, while soldiers busy themselves unloading much-needed military matériel.

Above: Steam ships wait offshore at City Point, Virginia, as construction goes on in the foreground. The Union depot at City Point was massive, and allowed U. S. Grant to keep his army well supplied during his campaign in Virginia in 1864 and 1865. Of the ships pictured here, that in the center, the side-wheel steamer *S. R. Spaulding*, was utilized as both a troop transport and hospital ship.

Above right: The Union gunboat *Mendota* patrols the James River. Built in Brooklyn and commissioned in May 1864, the *Mendota* was assigned to the James River Division of the North Atlantic Blockading Squadron. With her 10 guns, including two 100-pounder Parrott rifles, she supported the Union army's campaign against Richmond.

Lower right: Another Union gunboat on the James River. After Grant established his headquarters at City Point in 1864, Union gunboats vigilantly patrolled the river, ever on the lookout for Confederate batteries along the shore.

Above left: The double-turreted monitor *USS Onondaga* rests on the James River in 1864 or 1865. Another of the many Union warships that patrolled the James, the *Onondaga* saw action several times against Confederate batteries and ships guarding the Richmond approaches. After the war, the ship was sold to France and saw service in that nation's navy.

Left: The *USS Commodore Berry* was built in New York in 1859 as the ferry boat *Ethan Allen*. After the U.S. Navy purchased her in 1861, she was fitted with a 100-pounder rifle, three nine-inch smoothbore guns, and a 96-man crew. Though badly damaged in August 1863 by a Confederate mine on the James River, the *Commodore Berry* served until war's end.

Above: A Confederate David-type torpedo boat, abandoned in Charleston, South Carolina, after U.S. forces took the city in 1865. Built in that city from private funds in 1863, the original 50-foot-long *CSS David* operated on a steam engine, carried a crew of four, and was armed with a spar torpedo that extended from her bow. Though having the appearance of a submarine, the vessel did not submerge. In 1863 and 1864, the *CSS David* used her torpedo against several U.S. ships blockading Charleston Harbor.

AFRICAN AMERICANS

No one could have foreseen the wide-ranging roles that black-Americans would play in the Civil War. Nor could anyone have predicted the long-lasting effects that the war would have on race issues that linger even today. When the war began, nearly everyone in the North saw it as a struggle to preserve the Union. Abolitionists, however, believed a civil war was the best opportunity to abolish slavery.

The pivot point that vectored the war in the direction of ending slavery began with President Lincoln's Emancipation Proclamation, issued on January 1, 1863. He made the important document public after the strategic victory in Maryland the previous Fall at Antietam. The proclamation declared all slaves held within those states in rebellion free, though it did not attempt to abolish bondage within the boarder states, Tennessee, or Union-occupied swaths of land in other places across the South. The deft political move shifted the focus of the war while making it nearly impossible for England and France to enter the conflict on behalf of the Confederacy.

Slaves and free blacks alike took an active role in their own future. Many in bondage ran away, especially as Union armies began to penetrate into Southern territory. These contrabands often worked for Union armies by building fortifications, roads, driving wagons, and other important tasks. Others enlisted to fight against the Confederacy and served in many campaigns in regiments designated United Sates Colored Troops (USCT). The most famous black fighting regiment, the 54th Massachusetts, was led by Colonel Robert Gould Shaw in the suicidal charge against Battery Wagner, a desperate act of valor forever memorialized in the movie *Glory*.

Many blacks in the South voluntarily remained with their masters, tending the plantations and farms while the white men were fighting to keep them enslaved. Some accompanied their owners to the front as servants, and thousands more worked behind the lines as laborers. During the war's final weeks, the Confederacy officially agreed to enlist blacks to fight in exchange for their freedom, but nothing came of the effort before the war drew to its fitful close.

Right: A family of slaves from Beaufort, South Carolina, poses for the camera in 1862 after Union forces occupied the town.

Right: Timothy O'Sullivan snapped this remarkable image of a group of fugitive slaves fording the Rappahannock River in 1862. Thousands of slaves throughout the South fled to Union army lines in search of freedom during the war. Early on, their fate often relied upon the attitudes of the soldiers they encountered. Conservative Union officers might bar fleeing slaves from their camps, whereas those with an abolitionist bent might welcome them, even protecting them from slave catchers looking to return them to captivity.

Left: Soldiers of Company E, 4th United States Colored Troops. Though black men were barred from service in the U.S. Army at the outbreak of the war, a number of circumstances soon placed pressure on the policy. By May 1862, Union generals stationed in Missouri and South Carolina had issued proclamations that emancipated slaves in their departments. President Abraham Lincoln revoked both decrees, stating that the generals had exceeded their authority. But as the war ground on that summer, sagging volunteerism among whites and an unrelenting flow of fugitive slaves helped push Lincoln and the U.S. Congress to reconsider the subject. The resulting Confiscation Acts and Emancipation Proclamation opened the door for black military service. Volunteers of color flooded in; by war's end, roughly 180,000 black men served as soldiers, some ten percent of the Union army.

Above: A group of men–likely former slaves–sits on board the deck of a U.S. ship. Unlike the army, the U.S. Navy had a history of allowing blacks to serve in white crews; as early as the war's first summer, contrabands began to enlist for duty aboard military vessels. An estimated 18,000 black men served in the Union navy during the war.

Above right: A group of black soldiers strikes a proud pose. Blacks who served in the army faced discrimination, both from their comrades and the government. Until Congress acted in 1864, black soldiers were paid less than their white comrades.

Right: Black children stand in line outside a contraband school. During the war, northern abolitionists traveled southward to assist recently liberated slaves in areas secured by the Union army. The schools established by these volunteers offered former slaves of all ages the opportunity to learn how to read and write, among other things.

Above left: A group of black teamsters in camp at Bermuda Hundred, Virginia, in 1864. As teamsters, these men drove the mules and horses that hauled the army's supply wagons.

Left: Two contraband slaves pose outside an army tent. Many former slaves found employment in Union army regiments as personal servants, usually to individual officers or groups of enlisted men, often tent mates.

Above: A black cook tends to his pots in camp at City Point, Virginia. Many contraband slaves found steady work as cooks in Union army camps, either for entire companies or for smaller groups of soldiers.

Overleaf: Black laborers congregate on a wharf on the James River. The federal government put black men to work at a variety of important but menial jobs, including the construction of trenches and fortifications. In the South, the Confederate government regularly pressed slaves into such non-military service.

Above: These contrabands worked for the Union army chopping wood. In lieu of tents, they constructed earthen huts in the woods they worked.

Right: Freed black slaves pose for the camera in Richmond, Virginia. When a victorious President Lincoln entered the former Confederate capital in April 1865, the city's black residents enthusiastically crowded about him, eager to get an up-close look at "Father Abraham."

WONDERS OF ENGINEERING

Engineers played a critically important–and yet long overlooked–role in the American Civil War. Many were the most famous generals of the war–most of whom trained at an institution with its genesis six decades before the Civil War broke out.

In 1802, Congress authorized President Jefferson to organize a corps of engineers, which "shall be stationed at West Point, New York," and "shall constitute a military academy." The institution, of course, became what we know today as The United States Military Academy at West Point. The young graduating officers went on to serve in a wide variety of capacities in the cavalry, infantry, and artillery. The foundation of their education was grounded in engineering, a specialty deemed of crucial importance to a young country in both inland and coastal development.

The Civil War demonstrated the importance and reliability of West Point-trained officers in all matters of engineering. Some of the most obvious examples of their work entail the construction and maintenance of railroad trestles, bridges, docking facilities, roads, fortifications, and siege lines.

But the list of contributions does not stop there. Engineers operating with field armies routinely provided critical assistance by helping determine marching routes, constructing corduroy roads, and selecting positions upon which to deploy armed forces. Engineers generally had a keen sense of terrain, which often played a key role in determining the winner and loser of individual combats. One of the most prominent examples of this took place on July 2, 1863, at Gettysburg, where an 1850 graduate of West Point took decisive action that likely averted disaster. That afternoon, Gouverneur K.Warren, the Army of the Potomac's Chief Engineer, recognized the importance of holding Little Round Top on the distance southern end of the field. His keen eye and energetic effort siphoned off passing infantry to the high ground, guaranteeing that Union troops occupied the rocky heights just minutes in advance of attacking Confederate troops. The pictures that follow show some of the engineering highlights of the war that often go unrecognized.

Right: A group of Union soldiers with their wives and girlfriends stand at the end of one of engineer Herman Haupt's quick-build bridges made from pre-constructed sections.

Left: This photograph shows the impressive Chain Bridge, a heavy wooden cross-beam structure that spanned the Potomac River, connecting Washington, D.C. to Virginia. From the start of the war, Union soldiers and cannon vigilantly protected its approaches, through which countless troops passed—both on their way to the front and on retreat back to the capital.

Above: The Long Bridge, which connected Alexandria, Virginia, to Washington, D.C. Like the Chain Bridge, Union forces maintained a constant presence on and around the Long Bridge, whose approaches were protected by a series of forts. At night, the bridge's planks were taken up (as shown in this image) to prevent crossing by hostile forces.

Left: Scores of repaired railroad wheels and axles sit ready for use at a Union depot along the James River in Virginia. Both sides relied heavily on railroads to transport troops and supplies across long distances. The wear and tear of frequent use—along with damage inflicted by enemy saboteurs and roving cavalry— created a heavy workload for Union and Confederate repair crews, who often needed to work with haste to fix damaged cars and track. To deal quickly and efficiently with Confederate-inflicted damage to their lines, the U.S. stockpiled railroad materials at various locations throughout the country.

Above left: The Aqueduct Bridge, in Georgetown, whose pipes furnished Washington, D.C. with its water supply. Designed by Quartermaster General Montgomery C. Meigs, this bridge, like others that crossed into the federal capital, was protected by a series of defenses.

Left: Union soldiers crowd along on the banks of the Pamunkey River at the landing at White House, Virginia, home to a major supply depot for the Union army. Engineers erected the impressive system of docks pictured here, at which a steady stream of ships arrived to unload much-needed goods.

Above: Engineers from Major General Irvin McDowell's command work to construct a bridge over the north fork of the Rappahannock River near Sulphur Springs in August 1862. Engineers on both sides often had to work quickly and under pressure—and sometimes under enemy fire. Bridges damaged in battle or on purpose by a retreating army necessitated repair, whereas new structures were often needed to accommodate the needs of an advancing force.

Left: Union soldiers pose atop Woodbury's Bridge, which spanned the Chickahominy River in Virginia. During the Peninsular Campaign in 1862, Union engineers worked feverishly to build this structure and surrounding roads to allow George McClellan's army to continue its advance toward Richmond. The conditions proved rough—swampy land, reptiles, and flooding rains—but the engineers eventually completed the structure.

Left: Another view of the Union bridge erected over the Chickahominy River. Though relatively docile and easy to cross during dry weather, the Chickahominy River and swamp flooded easily, making crossing extremely difficult, as McClellan's men learned during the campaign for Richmond in 1862. That May, Confederates attempted to crush two Union corps temporarily cut off from the main army by the flooded Chickahominy, in what was known as the Battle of Seven Pines.

Above: One of the countless number of railroad bridges erected during the Civil War. Engineers were called upon frequently to build and repair such structures, which allowed vital supplies to reach troops as they operated farther and farther away from their base.

Left: Union engineers use roughly cut logs, underbrush, and earth to construct the Grape Vine Bridge over the Chickahominy River in 1862. During the Battle of Fair Oaks, Union soldiers under Major General Edwin Sumner's II Corps used the bridge to cross the rain-swollen river on their way to the fight. The weight of the passing troops was said to have stabilized the teetering structure, which collapsed in the rushing water soon after the men were safely across.

Left: The trestle bridge across the Cumberland Ravine at Whiteside, Tennessee, stands as a testament to the resourcefulness of Civil War engineers. Charged with erecting the structure with all speed, Union engineers looked high and low for sufficient materials, cutting down trees and even removing boards from the mill by the mountain torrent. When they were finished, all that remained of the mill, as shown here, was a skeletal frame.

Above and overleaf: Two views of the wooden bridge over the Tennessee River built by Union engineers during the campaign for Chattanooga in the fall of 1863. A system of pulley ropes operated a draw, which opened to allow passing ships through. Note the sentry posts that flank the entrance. When completed, the sturdy structure afforded the advancing Union army easy passage.

Above: Union engineers had to rebuild this bridge, on the Nashville and Chattanooga Railroad at Bridgeport, Alabama, on three occasions after Confederate forces damaged the structure during the Chattanooga Campaign. Spanning the Tennessee River, the bridge also included a wagon-way underneath the railroad trestles that accommodated the Union army's horse- and mule-drawn supply train.

Right: Probably Mathew Brady (in his characteristic long white coat) and anonymous fellow adventurers strike a precarious pose atop an unknown bridge. By war's end, building such structures–large and small–had become routine to army engineers. Note the blockhouse at one end, in which troops were stationed to guard the entrance to the structure.

Above: The High Bridge over the Appomattox River near Farmville, Virginia, was a source of contention between the opposing armies during Robert E. Lee's retreat from Petersburg in April 1865. Confederate engineers were ordered to destroy the structure after their comrades were safely across. The fires they started were extinguished by the lead element of the advancing Union army before they could do serious damage. The rebel engineers who attempted to finish the job came under enemy fire, which killed some and wounded others.

Right: A boy sits on horseback in the shadow of the fortified railroad bridge across the Cumberland River at Nashville, Tennessee. Union engineers under the command of Brigadier General Orlando M. Poe constructed the bridge after U.S. forces occupied the city in early 1862. This image is believed to have been taken in 1864 as Lieutenant General John Bell Hood's Confederate Army of Tennessee battled Major General George H. Thomas's Union force nearby.

Left: A military pontoon bridge spans the James River at Varina Landing in Virginia. Such bridges were an effective way to get men and materiel across wide waters in short order. Many such bridges were often destroyed or broken down after use, lest the enemy gain use of them.

Left: This image of the pontoon bridge across Appomattox Creek in Virginia reveals its simplicity of design. A series of pontoons—low, flat-bottom boats—are lashed together to form a base, over which a path of wooden planks has been laid. The resulting structure was flexible, permitting it to move with the water's current. Some pontoon bridges were constructed with a movable draw, able to open in order to let passing vessels through.

Above: Two wooden pontoon boats sit atop the wheeled wagons used to transport them. As the armies traveled, so did their pontoons, ready to be deployed as needed. The sturdy boats were 31-feet long and heavy, perfect for use when a wide river required crossing. For smaller jobs, shorter canvas pontoons might be used. These were much lighter and therefore easier to transport and work with.

Left: Union engineers constructed this canal aqueduct during the siege of Petersburg, Virginia, 1864-1865.

Right: This image shows the signal tower at Cobb's Hill, Virginia, in 1864. The 125-foot-high structure afforded its occupants a commanding view of the vicinity of Petersburg, so much so that Confederates erected a battery nearby in an attempt to destroy it. Note the soldiers perched at the highest level of the tower; one carries a signal flag, which was utilized to communicate with distant sections of the army.

TRAINS & TRANSPORTATION

In 1850, the United States had about 9,000 miles of railroad track. A decade later at the outbreak of the Civil War, more than 30,000 miles of wooden ties, banked earth, and forged iron rails crisscrossed the states. However, only 8,500 miles had been laid in the states that would eventually side with the Confederacy, leaving more than 22,000 miles in Northern hands. Many people on both sides of the Mason-Dixon Line did not fully recognize the importance of these numbers, and how they would affect the course of the war.

Railroads made it easier and more efficient to transfer large numbers of men, machinery, and supplies long distances, from New England all the way west to Ohio and then south into Kentucky, Tennessee, and beyond. Concerned more with making a profit than helping win the war, Northern railroads did not immediately cooperate with the Lincoln administration. Under the Railways and Telegraph Act of 1862, Lincoln seized individual lines and the War Department supervised them. Those few railroads directly affected were organized into the United States Military Railroad (U.S.M.R.R.).

The Confederacy had the advantage of interior lines, but its capacity to effectively use its railroads was severely hampered by a paucity of rolling stock, varying track gauges, the loss of skilled personnel, and the failure of many lines to actually link up in cities. The only direct line that connected Richmond, Virginia, to the Western Confederacy was through Chattanooga, Tennessee. Once this line was severed, the South had to move its armies and supplies down the eastern seaboard in a circuitous loop into the Confederate heartland.

Thousands of wagons and horses also hauled everything needed by the armies, and carried wounded men away from battlefields. The weather, road conditions, and availability of fodder to feed the animals directly affected the reliability of this means of transportation.

Right: Engine Number 133, United States Military Railroad, sits at the station at City Point, Virginia. During the war, the U.S. Army constructed countless miles of new rail lines as their forces campaigned across the young country.

Above: U.S. Military Engine Number 156, built in 1864. In early 1862, the U.S. War Department established a bureau responsible for the construction and operation of military railroads. At its head was native Philadelphian and West Point graduate Herman Haupt, chief engineer of the Pennsylvania Railroad before the war. Haupt's pioneering work allowed the Union army to use the railroads to their advantage, transporting men and supplies wherever and whenever they were needed. Rejecting a promotion to brigadier general in 1862, Haupt left the service the following year.

Right: Union soldiers congregate on a section of the Orange and Alexandria Railroad line near Union Mills, Virginia. The nearby railroad bridge that took the track across Bull Run was destroyed and rebuilt seven times during the war.

Left: Taken soon after the Battle of Antietam in September 1862, this photograph shows the bridge that extended the Sharpsburg-to-Boonsboro turnpike over Antietam Creek. One of three bridges that spanned the creek, Confederates–including Robert E. Lee–used this "Middle Bridge" to cross into town as they prepared to confront Major General George McClellan's approaching Army of the Potomac. During the fighting of the 17th, this bridge marked the center of the Union position, near where McClellan's reserve forces were positioned. Though the Middle Bridge did not see the heavy fighting that the nearby Rohrbach (Lower) Bridge did, the scars of battle are still clearly seen in the destroyed fencing and stone wall.

Above: This image of Stoneman's Station on the Aquia Creek and Fredericksburg Railroad shows neatly stacked commissary stores awaiting transport to Union soldiers. Such spots bustled with activity during the war as army quartermasters performed the constant duty of keeping their men well supplied. Not pictured is Stoneman's sizeable government bakery that produced bread for the troops.

Left: Workers pose alongside spare train parts at this railroad repair shop. At great cost, the federal government established many such repair depots during the war so as to keep its trains, wagons, and wheel-carried weapons in operating condition.

Overleaf: This photograph shows Hanover Junction, Pennsylvania, as it appeared during the war. The junction marked the spot where the Northern Central Railway met the Hanover Branch Railroad, the latter traveling toward Gettysburg. After the Battle of Gettysburg in July 1863, wounded Union soldiers crowded the junction as they awaited transfer to various hospitals. That November, the train carrying President Lincoln, on his way to deliver the Gettysburg Address, stopped over here.

Left: A U.S. military train on the tracks at City Point, Virginia. During the campaigns of 1864 and 1865, trains ran from the Union army's massive supply depot at City Point to Lieutenant General U. S. Grant's lines outside Petersburg, Virginia, shuttling troops and supplies to the front.

Above: The job of a military railroad man was not entirely safe. In this photograph, men point to damage to the U.S. military engine "Fred Leach" created by Confederate shot. The engine came under enemy fire on August 1, 1863, as it was running on the Orange and Alexandria Railroad.

Above: Union Soldiers in North Anna, Virginia survey the extensive damage to the bridge of the Richmond and Fredericksburg Railroad in May 1864.

Right: A group of laborers works to repair the single-track railroad at Mufreesboro, Tennessee after the Battle of Stones River.

Left: A train of U.S. Army wagons crowds the road into downtown Petersburg, Virginia. These were the first Union wagons to enter the embattled town after its fall to U. S. Grant's forces during the first days of April 1865. Grant's siege of the vital Confederate city began the previous summer; for ten months, the opposing armies fought each other to a bloody stalemate from their elaborate systems of earthworks and trenches. By the time Robert E. Lee's withdrew his forces, total casualties for both sides had exceeded 70,000– killed, wounded, or captured. Grant's advantage in men and matériel–and his ability to supply his army whenever needed–was a key component to his ultimate victory.

RUINS

Every war kills people, destroys property and buildings, and scars the landscape, and the Civil War was no different. As one noted historian described it, the war was fought in 10,000 places, claimed 600,000 lives, and left much of South in ruins. According to some calculations, the Confederacy suffered $10,000,000,000 in property loss and half of its livestock was eaten, captured, killed, or driven away.

Ruins, loss, and its attendant human despair were delivered in numerous ways. Armies rampaged across the countryside destroying crops, ruining fences, and cleaning out farms of their produce and livestock. Cavalrymen ripped up railroads, pulling out the track and wrapping the heated iron rails around trees to form "Sherman's neckties." The twisted iron was named after General William T. Sherman, who employed the practice in his infamous March to the Sea.

Entire cities suffered the hand of war, but few as completely as Richmond, Virginia–the permanent capital of the short-lived Confederacy. When General Robert E. Lee's army lost its defensive grip on Petersburg and Richmond on April 1, 1865, he sent President Davis a telegram the following morning: "I think it is absolutely necessary that we should abandon our position tonight." He left a swath of destruction in his wake none of Richmond's citizens could have foreseen in the heady days of 1861. Fires raged out of control, burning a large section of Richmond to the ground. Streets were littered with glass, wood, and twisted metal. Bridges, once so critical to the Confederacy for moving troops and supplies, lie broken and smoldering in the James River, whose muddy banks included the remnants of ships and the holed smokestack of a recently destroyed Confederate ironclad.

This image was replayed in many parts of the Old South. With its economy in ruins and a large percentage of its male population dead, these states suffered hardship for several generations, and are only now beginning to fully recover. Fortunately for posterity, some of this desolation was captured by Mathew Brady in a series of stark photographs that allow the reader the chance to ponder the cost of war.

Right: Fredericksburg, Virginia, shows the scars of battle. During the fighting that took place here in December 1862, Union forces shelled the town before entering it, fighting the occupying Confederates street by street as they advanced.

Above: The Phillips House in Fredericksburg, Virginia, which Major General Ambrose Burnside, commander of the Army of the Potomac, used as his headquarters during the battle there. Burnside laid the plans for what turned out to be the disastrous defeat of December 13, 1862, in this house; during the fighting on the 13th, the Union army suffered over 12,000 casualties, most in the futile attempt to dislodge Robert E. Lee's Confederates from the heights west of town. The damage to the Phillips House seen here was caused after the battle, in February 1863, when the structure caught fire.

Above right: The ruins of Gaines's Mill, around which Union and Confederate forces clashed during the Peninsular Campaign of 1862. Robert E. Lee lost approximately 8,000 men during the engagement, the third of the so-called Seven Days Battles. His opponent, George McClellan, lost around 7,000 in defeat.

Right: A Union soldier stands beside the riddled smokestack of the *CSS Virginia II* in this late-war photograph. The 197-foot ironclad ram served on the James River, where it engaged the Union fleet on several occasions. The *Virginia II* incurred heavy damage during fighting in January 1865; as Union forces approached Richmond that April, Confederates destroyed her lest she be captured.

Left: As this photograph shows, little remained of the Richmond and Petersburg Railroad bridge over the James River at war's end. Confederates destroyed the structure as they withdrew from Petersburg in April 1865.

Right: This interior shot of Fort Pulaski in Georgia reveals some of the significant damage it incurred during fighting in April 1862. Union forces bombarded the Confederate fort for 30 hours before it fell. Though the masonry structure was damaged heavily, only one member of its Confederate garrison was killed during the engagement.

Below: The arsenal in Richmond, Virginia, stood in ruins at war's end, destroyed during the evacuation fire set by the retreating Confederates in April 1865.

Right, below, and opposite page: These images show the extent of the damage Richmond suffered at war's end. The city that had served as the capital of the Confederacy and bustled with activity throughout the war came to a quick and devastating end soon after the news arrived on April 2, 1865, that Lee's lines at Petersburg had broken. Many residents fled in haste, businesses were plundered, and the city's munitions stores fired. The resulting conflagration burned much of the city's commercial district to the ground.

INDEX

ACKNOWLEDGMENTS

I must thank Colin Gower for his faith in handing me this project. It has been a good experience.

Terry Johnston, the editor of an outstanding collection of letters by University of South Carolina Press entitled *Him on the One Side and Me on the Other: The Civil War Letters of Alexander Campbell, 79th New York Infantry Regiment, and James Campbell, 1st South Carolina Battalion* (1999), provided extraordinary assistance with the captions. I have worked with Terry on a number of projects, and have enjoyed each of them. Eric Wittenberg graciously agreed to pen the Foreword. Eric is the author of a number of outstanding titles, including the newly released *One Continuous Fight: The Retreat from Gettysburg* and the *Pursuit of Lee's Army of Northern Virginia, July 4 - 14, 1863* (with J. D. Petruzzi and Mike Nugent) and the wildly popular 2006 release of *Plenty of Blame to Go Around: Jeb Stuart's Controversial Ride to Gettysburg* (with J. D. Petruzzi). Both men contributed mightily to this work.

Anne Lang–Picture Research

The National Archive